Trinity Dogma
The Book

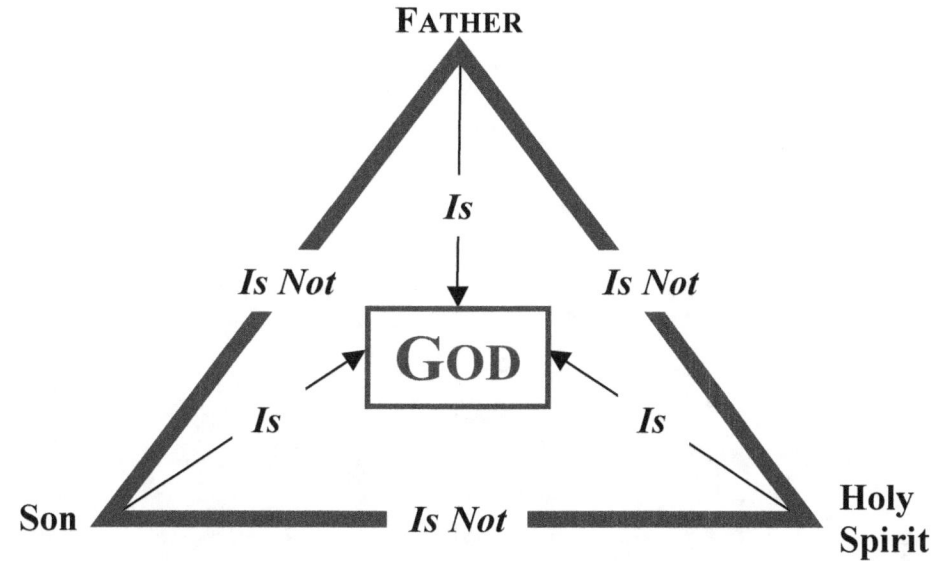

Copyright 2009
Rev. Edward G. Palmer
All Rights Reserved

Trinity Dogma
The Book

Copyright Notice

Thank you for purchasing "Trinity Dogma - The Book." Copyright laws protect this written work of Reverend Edward G. Palmer. Distribution to others in any form is a violation of copyright laws. Volume discounts are available. Contact the author for further details. Thank you for respecting copyright laws. God will bless your honesty. This work is a ministry to Christians with God's message that they need to love HIS Word more than they love the doctrines of their Church.

Copyright 2009
Rev. Edward G. Palmer
All Rights Reserved

Trinity Dogma

Copyright © 2009 by Edward G. Palmer
Published by JVED Publishing
Elk River, Minnesota 55330

    ISBN 978-0-9768833-6-4 (Trinity Dogma - The Book)

Palmer, Edward G.
    1. Faith—The Apostle Edward 2. Bible Prophecy—Christian Mythology
    3. Christianity—Trinity Doctrine

Printed in the United States of America.

All rights reserved. No portion of this book may be reproduced in any form without the written permission of the Author.

Notice. This book and its entire contents represents the sole opinion of Reverend Edward G. Palmer based upon his thirty plus years of in-depth Bible studies, his actual life experiences, his personal diaries and publicly available documents including religious ecumenical documents. No part of this book is intended to offer professional counseling of any type. Persons involved in cultic churches, those in need of spiritual counseling, religious or any other professional advice should seek competent professional help.

Capitalization Protocol. On all Bible citations, regardless of the translation used, and where the context clearly points to God Almighty or to Jesus Christ, this book makes the distinction between the two by using either small cap characters or lower case characters. For God Almighty, a small capitalized style protocol is followed and reflected in the format: CREATOR, FATHER, GIVER, HE, HIS, HIM, HIMSELF, YOU, YOUR, ME, MINE, MOST HIGH, MY, MYSELF, LORD and SAVIOR, ETC. For Jesus Christ, a lower case protocol is used except for Lord and Son. Hence, when these pronouns are used for Jesus, they show up as: he, his, him, himself, you, your, me, my, myself, savior, Lord, or Son. This has generally been followed throughout the book, but is not the case with every cited verse. It is used for those verses in which the context cannot be easily disputed or in the case of citing a quality or attribute, which belongs solely to God. For those interested in the original translation capitalization, the author refers them to the actual Bible version used for the cited text. A list of Bible translations is shown on the next page. In some other cases, capital letters used within the cited sentence structure were also changed on common words for ease of reading or modern grammar. In other cases, the capitalized letters were left as shown in the original translation. Hence the original Bible phrase "; Because" might appear as "; because." In all instances, Apostle Edward maintains complete integrity of translation and the writings herein can be traced back to the original Bibles to confirm the accuracy of presentation. While not perfect, the capitalization protocol is fairly consistent and enhances the reading and value of Apostle Edward's teachings.

Translation Notice & Bible Definitions

The following Bible translations were researched for this book along with three Hebrew texts and one or more ancient manuscripts such as the Book of Enoch (ENO). Except where otherwise indicated and in regards to capitalization of words, all Scripture quotations are taken from the Holy Bible, New King James Version © 1979, 1980, 1982 by Thomas Nelson, Inc., Publishers. Verses that are followed by a two, three or four-letter capitalized identifier are from the following Bible translations or reference works.

Abbreviation	Bible Definition
KJV; NKJV	King James Version [1]; New King James Version [2]
AMP	Amplified Bible [3]
ASB; NASB	American Standard [4]; New American Standard Bible [5]; +1977v [6]
BBE	Bible In Basic English [7]
CEV	Contemporary English Version [8]
DB	Darby Bible [9]
DR	Douay-Rheims 1957 Catholic Bible [10]
ENO	Book of Enoch — Richard Laurence 1883 Edition [11]
ESV	English Standard Version [12]
GEN	Geneva Bible [13]
GN; GNA	Good News [14]; Good News Apocrypha [15]-Today's English Bible
GW	God's Word Bible [16]
HEB	Hebrew Bible — English Translation JPS 1917 Edition [17]
HOL	Holman Christian Standard Bible [18]
ICB	International Children's Bible [19]
JSB	Jewish Study Bible [20] - Jewish Publication Society 1985, 1999
LIV; NLT	Living Bible [21]; New Living Translation [22]
MB	MicroBible [23]
MES	The Message [24]
MLT	Morris Literal Translation [25]
MOF	James Moffatt Translation, Final Edition [26]
NAB	New American Bible 1991 - Catholic Bible [27]
NET	New English Translation [28]
NIV	New International Version [29]
NCV	New Century Version [30]
NJB	New Jerusalem Bible [31]
PNT	Phillips New Testament Bible [32]
REB	Revised English Bible [33]
RSV; NRSV	Revised Standard Version [34]; New Revised Standard Version [35]
SET	Simple English Translation [36]
TAN	Tanach - The Stone Edition 1996 [37]
TB	Transliterated Bible [38]
WEB	Webster's Bible [39]
WES	Wesley New Testament [40]
WEY	Weymouth's NT [41]
YLT	Young's Literal Translation [42]

Trinity Dogma © 2009 Rev. Edward G. Palmer

Table of Contents

Copyright Notice	ii-iii
Translation Notice & Bible Definitions	iv
Trinity Dogma Subjects	v-vi
Foreword	vii
You need to hear God	viii
You need to hear Jesus	ix
Ten teachings of Jesus	ix-ix
Jesus identifies God	xi
Paul identifies God	xi
You are mistaken not knowing Scripture	1-4
First two lessons from God's Word	5
Third lesson from God's Word	6
FATHER is the God identified in New Testament	7-8
Is Jesus a liar?	9
Worship only the God Jesus identified	10
Christ says he was the first creation of God	11
Discussion of Scripture	12-13
Paul's teaching about God and Christ	14
Antichrist spirit teaches against Christ's humanity	15
Jesus was made a human like all other humans	16
Lessons four through thirty-eight	17-18
God is not a man nor as the son of man	18-19
Sons of God	19-20
Jesus as God's Apostle and High Priest	20
Jesus as God's Prophet	21-22
Jesus as seed of David in the flesh	23
Jesus as Son of God in the Spirit	23
Jesus as angel of God	23
Jesus as archangel of God	23
Jesus as our spiritual rock	24
Jesus instructions on prayer	24-25
Seven teachings of Jesus	25
Don't add or subtract from God's Word	26
Warning from the Book of Enoch	26
Lessons thirty-nine through seventy-six	27-28
Trinity Dogma is the great End-Times deception	28-33
End-Times warning	29
How to know the truth	30-31
Bible prophecy fulfilled	32
Judgment begins in house of God	33
Thirty-three Scriptures from God "to hear"	34-35
Lessons seventy-seven through one hundred-seven	36-37
Church money grabbing tradition	37-38
Church carved image tradition	38-42

Trinity Dogma © 2009 Rev. Edward G. Palmer

The missing second commandment	42
An outside view of Catholic Mass	43-44
Be still to know God	44
Jesus and Paul teach FATHER is God - Table	45
God the FATHER Scripture search	46-47
Who knew that God was *only* the FATHER? - List	47
The gospel Jesus taught to Paul	48
Don't interpret Scripture using trinity doctrine	49-51
Two soul stealing Church traditions	52
Lessons one hundred-eight to one-hundred-sixty	53-55
The Apostle's Creed and discussion	55-58
The Roman Pantheon - Table	59-61
A summary of Roman history	61-68
The trinity doctrine was not created in a vacuum	68
Twenty-two lessons from Roman history	69-70
Constantine converts to Arianism on his deathbed	70-71
Tertullian coins "trinity"	71
The Athanasian Creed and discussion	72-77
Twenty-five salvation truths	74
The deceivers & the deceived	78
The Church as pillar of truth	78
Catholic basis of trinity doctrine	79
Commentary of trinity basis	80-81
Basic trinity timeline	81
The Catholic Profession of Faith in 2009	82
Scripture errors in Catholic Profession of Faith	83
Work out your salvation	84
You are misled and like angels	84
Get your praise from God	84
Is your brain wired for social conformity?	85
You need to love truth and renew your mind	86-87
The few and the many	87
Jesus laid no claim to equality with God	88
Jesus was human like you and I - Table	89-90
Trinitarian Church lies and it does not know God	90
Edward, what if you are mistaken?	91
And, what if I am right?	91
Conclusion	92-94
Appendix A - A real salvation prayer	95-96
Appendix B - Baptism doctrine	97-98
Appendix C - Thomas' exclamation	99-100
Appendix D - Catholics & the Bible	101-107
Notes	108-111
Index & Bible Verse Cross Reference	112-124
Apostle Edward asks, "Are you ready?"	125
Free Newsletter & Contact Information	126-130

Foreword

What is missing in Christianity that could cause 50% of Christians to vote on each side of the political spectrum in elections? With literally half of all *named* Christians supporting policies like abortion on demand, gay marriage, confiscatory tax policies and the forced redistribution of wealth by governments? If you think God or HIS only begotten human Son Jesus Christ would support these and similar policies, you are at the least, ignorant of Scripture and even worse, may be "programmed" by church dogma. This is doctrine from a church, which no longer respects God's Word and holds HIS Word in lower esteem than the writings of their own councils of men and women. Listen, God respects your freedom to choose. HIS respect for our free will is expressed in Scripture at Revelation 22:11.

Free will means each and every one of us has the freedom to choose what we will or will not believe. It goes to say without question that, since God respects our free will, you and your church should also respect everyone's free will. Can you love like God does if you don't love someone unconditionally, respecting their freedom to believe as they choose? No, and you cannot love unconditionally as God does if you only love someone "as long as they will agree with the doctrines of your church." And, listen, if your religion forces its doctrines upon people and suppresses their freedom to challenge, question, and openly discuss and explore in depth church beliefs supposedly based upon Holy Scripture against that Holy Scripture —then such religion or church is not of God. It's that simple, because God HIMSELF tells us we can come and reason with HIM in Isaiah 1:18. If we can go and reason directly with God ALMIGHTY, then why would any church or religious leader shut down debate? They wouldn't if they were truly of God!

The answer to the question posed in the first paragraph, is that people now routinely esteem their own opinion or their churches doctrine above that of the written and inspired word of God as shown in the Holy Bible. Many churches even actively teach against the Scripture they claim is the basis of their belief system. Ergo, look at what they do and not at what they say and you will know them: remember? Jesus said, "You will know them by their fruits." So, what is being taught by many religions and denominations is often dogma, which is not of God and is unsupported by Holy Scripture. The most pernicious and evil of the dogmas is that of the trinity doctrine adopted by the Catholic Church in 325 AD. It is now accepted without challenge or debate throughout most of Christianity. To even challenge the trinity doctrine and idea of a triune god is to get one labeled as a heretic. Yes, even I have felt the weight of family and friends who believe I may be the ultimate heretic. I have been persecuted for my stand on God's Word and have even lost the love of those who are dear to me; people who have never learned how to love others unconditionally as God does. Yet, it is they and not I who ignore God's Word and the simple teachings of HIS only human begotten Son, our Lord Jesus Christ.

So let me take you on a journey through Scripture and Roman history. It is my prayer that God will open your mind and heart up so you can hear, understand, and *then* obey HIM.

Do you hear God? What about Jesus, do you hear him?

Trinity Dogma © 2009 Rev. Edward G. Palmer

You Need To Hear God!

Jesus said: "Whoever belongs to God hears the words of God; for this reason you do not listen, because you do not belong to God."
John 8:47 (NAB)

This means reading and studying the Holy Bible, which are "the words of God."

"While [Jesus] was speaking, a woman from the crowd called out and said to him, 'Blessed is the womb that carried you and the breasts at which you nursed.' Jesus replied, 'Rather, blessed [more so] are those who hear the word of God and observe it.' " Luke 11:27-28 (NAB)

Jesus taught us that even though Mary was blessed, being able to hear and obey the word of God makes you more blessed than Mary was. Catholics take note. This is the word of your Lord! The NKJV reads: But [Jesus] said, "More than that, blessed are those who hear the word of God and keep it!"

God's Word Is Important!

"All Scripture is inspired by God and is useful for teaching, for refutation, for correction, and for training in righteousness, so that one who belongs to God may be competent, equipped for every good work." 2 Timothy 3:16-17 (NAB)

If you belong to God, you must study God's Word. It will equip you for every good work.

God's Word Can Save Your Soul!

"Therefore, put away all filth and evil excess and humbly welcome the word [of God] that has been planted in you and is able to save your souls." James 1:21 (NAB)

If you think going to Mass or some other aspect of your church will save you, this is not what the Bible teaches. It is the word of God "planted in you" that is "able to save your soul." Think about this the next time you are taught not to read the Bible, because you won't understand it. Then tell whoever says this to you that you can understand the Word.

You Can Understand The Word!

"Therefore, do not continue in ignorance, but try to understand what is the will of the Lord." Ephesians 5:17 (NAB)

Paul said, "When you read this you can understand my insight into the mystery of Christ." Ephesians 3:4 (NAB)

Trinity Dogma © 2009 Rev. Edward G. Palmer

"For we write you nothing but what you can read and understand, and I hope that you will understand completely." 2 Corinthians 1:13 (NAB)

"We also know that the Son of God [Jesus] has come and has given us discernment [an ability to understand] to know the ONE [FATHER] who is true. And we are in the ONE [FATHER] who is true, [if we are truly] in HIS Son Jesus Christ. HE [the FATHER] is the [one and only] true God and eternal life." 1 John 5:20 (NAB)

"Then [Jesus] opened their minds to understand the scriptures." Luke 24:45 (NAB)

You can understand God's Word if you will open up your heart and simply read it in the simple language that it was written in. You don't have to excuse away Scripture because it teaches against your church's doctrine. You simply accept Scripture and understand that it is the church that doesn't understand God when it teaches against HIS Word. Don't read into Scripture that which is not stated clearly. Let God's Word speak for itself!

You Need To Hear Jesus!

"While [Peter] was still speaking, behold, a bright cloud cast a shadow over them, then from the cloud came a voice [from God] that said, 'This is my beloved Son, with whom I am well pleased; listen to him.' " Matthew 17:5 (NAB)

God HIMSELF commands us to listen to HIS only human begotten Son Jesus Christ.

"Whoever teaches something different and does not agree with the sound words of our Lord Jesus Christ and the religious teaching is conceited, understanding nothing, and has a morbid disposition for arguments and verbal disputes. From these come envy, rivalry, insults, evil suspicions, and mutual friction among people with corrupted minds, who are deprived of the truth, supposing religion to be a means of gain." 1 Timothy 6:3-6 (NAB)

Anyone who teaches opposite of what Jesus taught knows nothing about God's Word.

Ten Teachings Of Jesus

1. **God sent Jesus.**
    a. Matthew 10:40; 15:24
    b. Luke 4:18; 4:43; 9:48
    c. John 4:30; 5:24, 30, 36, 37, 38; John 6:29, 38, 39, 40, 44
       John 7:16, 18, 28, 29, 30
       John 8:16, 18, 26, 29, 42
       John 9:4; 10:26; 11:42; 12:44, 45
       John 12:49; 13:16, 20; 14:24
       John 15:21; 16:5; 17:3, 8, 18, 21; 17:25; 20:21
       Acts 3:26

2. God gave Jesus a purpose.

    a. Jesus said: "I must preach the kingdom of God to the other cities also, because for this purpose I have been sent [by God]." Luke 4:43

3. Jesus only did the will of God.

    a. Jesus said: "My food is to do the will of HIM who sent me, and to finish HIS work." John 4:34

4. Jesus did nothing on his own accord.

    a. Jesus said: "I can of myself do nothing. As I hear, I judge; and my judgment is righteous, because I do not seek my own will but the will of the FATHER who sent me." John 5:30

5. Jesus came from Heaven to do God's will.

    a. Jesus said: "For I have come down from Heaven, not to do my own will, but the will of HIM [God] who sent me." John 6:38

6. Jesus must perform the works of God.

    a. Jesus said: "I must work the works of HIM who sent me while it is day, the night is coming when no one can work." John 9:4

7. Jesus' doctrine was God's, not his own.

    a. Jesus said: "My doctrine is not mine, but HIS who sent me." John 7:16

8. God is greater than Jesus.

    a. Jesus said: "Most assuredly, I say to you, a servant is not greater than his master; nor is he [Jesus] who is sent greater than HE [God] who sent him." John 13:16

9. Jesus spoke God's Words, not his own.

    a. Jesus said: "He who does not love me does not keep my words; and the word which you hear is not mine, but the FATHER'S [God's] who sent me." John 14:24

10. Eternal life is to know Jesus' God.

    a. Jesus said: "And this is eternal life, that they may know YOU [God], the only true God, and Jesus Christ whom YOU have sent." John 17:3

Listen carefully. Can you hear Jesus Christ our Lord?

Trinity Dogma © 2009 Rev. Edward G. Palmer

Jesus Identifies The FATHER As God!

Jesus said: "But go to my brothers and tell them, 'I am going to my FATHER and your FATHER, to my God and your God.' " John 20:17 (NAB)

Warning To Stay In Jesus' Teachings!

John said: "Anyone who is so 'progressive' as not to remain in the teaching of the Christ does not have God; whoever remains in the teaching [of Jesus Christ] has the FATHER and the Son." 2 John 9 (NAB)

Paul said, "See to it that no one captivate you with an empty, seductive philosophy according to human tradition, according to the elemental powers of the world and not according to Christ." Colossians 2:8 (NAB)

Given the need to accept the teachings of our Lord Jesus Christ and not to teach against them [1 Timothy 6:3-5], will you accept Christ's teaching in John 20:17? That God's identity is our FATHER and that HE is our only God?

Paul Identifies The FATHER As God!

Paul said: "Yet for us there is one God, the FATHER, from WHOM all things are and for WHOM we exist, and one Lord, Jesus Christ, through whom all things are and through whom we exist." 1 Corinthians 8:6 (NAB)

Can you hear Jesus?
Are you listening to God's Word?

Trinity Dogma © 2009 Rev. Edward G. Palmer

Trinity Dogma
The Book

Trinity Dogma

Jesus answered and said to them, "You are mistaken, not knowing the Scriptures nor the power of God." Matthew 22:29 NKJV

And Jesus answering, said to them: "You err, not knowing the Scriptures, nor the power of God." Matthew 22:29 Douay-Rheims

> **dogma** :ˈdôgmə :
> Noun
> A principle or set of principles laid down by an authority as incontrovertibly true: *the Christian dogma of the Trinity* : *the rejection of political dogma.*
> ORIGIN mid 16th cent.: via late Latin from Greek ***dogma 'opinion,'*** from ***dokein 'seem good, think.'***

New Oxford American Dictionary, Apple OSX Dictionary Version 2.0.2 (51.4)

For 1684 years now [from 325 AD forward], the Church has taught a trinity dogma, asserting that Jesus Christ is God. This man-made doctrine is not found in the text of the Holy Bible. Instead, the Catholic Church created the doctrine, by consensus at the council of Nicea in 325 AD. In addition to creating the trinity doctrine, Scripture in some bibles has been altered by the Church to support the doctrine. Ergo, text in the Catholic *Douay-Rheims Bible* has been altered to support the trinity doctrine.

Text in other bibles or religious works such as the *New World Translation Bible* and the *Book of Mormon* have also been altered to reflect and support the sect's religious beliefs. Yet, many other bible translations reflect a genuine effort to translate ancient Hebrew or Greek into modern English and do not incorporate religious bias or dogma into the text. All modern *study* bibles incorporate support of the trinity dogma in their notes and outlines, as the dogma reflects the orthodox teaching that Jesus is God.

Putting it another way, if you do not believe that Jesus is God, many would not consider you to be a Christian. At very least, you would not be a member of orthodox Christianity.

It is not the purpose of this book to fully explain the trinity doctrine or how the Church rationalizes its dogma. Instead, I want to discuss what Jesus had to say about all of this. Of course, Jesus never mentioned the word trinity, nor will you find the word or concept defined within any Scripture. Yet, Jesus was not silent on who his God was and there is plenty to consider in his own teachings that actually dispel the notion that he was God.

C.S. Lewis, a renowned Christian apologist, once wrote that Jesus is God. After careful consideration, he came to this conclusion and commented in *Mere Christianity*: "If Jesus is not God, then we are all engaged in idolatry." Verily I say unto you that C.S. Lewis was wrong and that it is absolute truth, everyone who worships Jesus is engaged in idolatry.

It is my sincere prayer that you will be motivated to pick up a Bible and begin to study the Scriptures cited in this book. Only then can your heart and mind begin to submit to Scripture and learn to value Scripture over Church dogma.

> *Prayer: Our heavenly FATHER, the ONE and only true God, please open up the minds and hearts of all who read the words of this book so that they may understand the words that your only human begotten Son, Jesus Christ, gave to us. Help them to understand that Jesus only spoke and did what YOU told him to do. Help them to understand it was not YOU who came down to die on the cross for us, but YOU who sent Jesus Christ to us to guide us back to our heavenly home. Help all to understand the truth of YOUR Word so that they would not be "mistaken" about Scripture. And, it's my deepest prayer, FATHER, that those who read the words of this book would feel compelled by YOUR Spirit to open a Bible and begin their own study and search for spiritual truth. I pray, FATHER, that everyone would learn to place YOUR Holy Word above all Church dogma! Edward*

If you have read the *Seven Messages* that God has given me, it should be clear that Jesus is not God. Yet, I know that this may not be the case for many who are firm trinity believers. I communicated for months with a Christian woman in Chicago who had read the *Seven Messages* and still believed Jesus was God. By her own words she had been a Christian some 43 years from the age of 13. That is but one example of many. Even those I love are confused, having been programmed by Church dogma for years. For example, I love a wonderful Catholic woman who thoroughly believes that Jesus is God and by faith she accepts it as truth. She declares: "It's a mystery!" And, at every Catholic Mass, the Church reinforces and celebrates its so-called mystery of "God becoming a man."

As a result, millions of Christians now worship Jesus around the world. It's not just in the Catholic Church, but also in all orthodox Protestant churches. There can be no doubt that this Nicea documented man-made trinity doctrine is now Church dogma. A doctrine laid down by the [Mother] Church as "incontrovertibly true." The Church now requires that its trinity dogma be accepted on faith and must never be challenged. To do so is heretical and even blasphemous to the orthodox community. I would add, to deny the trinity is also very personally threatening to those who have spent decades believing it. Even I know!

Nowhere in Christendom is the idolatry more obvious than in the Catholic Church. At Mass, Catholics bow down and kneel to the image of the crucifix, which stands directly behind a hewed altar. Adjacent to the image of Jesus on the cross are images or statues of Mary and Joseph. This is idolatry in God's eyes and it is also a blatant violation of the second commandment HE gave us in Exodus 20:1-17 and Deuteronomy 5:6-21. I will discuss the second commandment in a few moments and demonstrate how the Church has altered God's commandments to accommodate its rituals and traditions. Yes, it is true that the Catholic Church has rationale for all of its religious practices including bowing and kneeling down to carved images, but will God excuse those who should know better? The Priests? The Bishops? The Cardinals? The Pope? No, HE won't!

Instead of Mary being honored as a woman who was blessed by God, Catholics actually revere her as the "Mother of God." *Fact*: Mary was the mother of Jesus, a human man, which the Bible fully documents. *Church dogma*: Jesus is God. *Church conclusion*: Mary is the "Mother of God." This is sheer apostasy when it comes to Scripture. And, it is an abomination to God; insulting to the human sacrifice that Christ suffered on the cross.

Instead of praying to the God that Jesus taught us to pray to, Catholics pray to Mary and a long list of Saints whom they beseech to become intercessors with God on their behalf. If it seems like I am picking on Catholics, I am not. Virtually all-orthodox churches have similar apostasies that they are engaged in that oppose the truth of God's Word. Yet, the Catholic Church is the "Mother" of all orthodox churches and has led the way in terms of apostate teachings about the nature of Jesus. Therefore, we will examine some teachings of Jesus using the *New King James Version* [Protestant] and *Douay-Rheims* [Catholic] bibles side by side. The Catholic *New American Bible* and others will be used as needed.

There are two primary objectives for this book. Everything I write will revolve around these two objectives. The first one should be obvious. I'd like to present further evidence from Scripture to you as to why Jesus is not God. I will discuss some things that Jesus himself has taught us. Second, I would like to challenge you to pick up a Bible and seek the truth for yourself. My objective here is to educate you about God's Holy Word and why you should use it as your basis for spiritual truth. I do not seek to teach you theories or to impart my opinion upon you. I seek to educate you about God's Word. These are two very distinctly different teachings. You've already listened to the opinions and dogma of the Church for many years. Isn't it now time for you to listen to the word of God?

> **"[Jesus] answered and said: It is written, 'Man shall not live by bread alone, but by every word that proceeds from the mouth of God.'"**
> **Matthew 4:4 (NKJV) [Note: This verse refers to Deuteronomy 8:3]**

> **"[Jesus] answered and said: It is written, not in bread alone doth man live, but in every word that proceedeth from the mouth of God."**
> **Matthew 4:4 (Douay-Rheims)**

I remember very distinctly a conversation God had with me while attending church many years ago. In fact, it was over 12 years ago. As I sat in the pew reading my Bible and studying the Scripture being discussed, the Pastor began to LIE. I listened intensely and with astonishment as he repeated his lie three more times. Each time he spoke, I followed along in my Bible looking at the word of God being discussed. The Pastor was lying about Scripture. The third time he repeated his lie, I heard the voice of God speaking to me. God said: "It is now time for you to choose Edward. It's either the Pastor's word or MY Word." Of course, I said: "It's YOUR Word FATHER!"

There is good reason why many churches do not want you to read your Bible. If you study it, you may come to the realization that you are being programmed with Church dogma and not with God's Word. Ultimately you will surrender to God's Word and refuse to accept any apostasy or you will close your mind to God and blindly follow the Church.

I do not know a single Orthodox Church that is not currently engaged in some form of idolatry or false teaching, which speaks against the written word of God. Does it really matter? Isn't there multiple truths depending on who interprets it? I will let you come to your own conclusions. However, if you base your salvation on the words of the Bible that your Church claims is God's Word — wouldn't you like to know what HIS words are? Yes, this is a trick question. If you have truly surrendered your heart and claim salvation through Christ, why wouldn't your heart want to seek out all of God's Word? Why wouldn't you want to know what pleases and displeases your LORD? Think about it.

If you do study the Bible and do surrender yourself to God's Word, you will eventually wind up leaving the doctrinal Church and will become one of the 20 million or more of us now in home churches or in the wilderness awaiting further instructions from God.

In the case of Bible selection, you will need either a *King James Version* (KJV) or *New King James Version* (NKJV) and two other popular translations to compare against each other. I would recommend the NKJV as your main Bible as it updates the old English used within the KJV. Note: The KJV old English is illustrated in the *Douay-Rheims'* bible verses shown in this book. The *New Revised Standard Version* (NRSV) is a good translation, which is generally unbiased, but still has nuances like Titus 2:13-14. I would also recommend getting a Parallel Bible in which multiple translations are compared side by side to each other. Studying with three or more bible translations will prevent you from becoming trapped by a translation error or the manipulation of text by translators. It will also eliminate the dogma promoted by any one denomination. Avoid study bibles and commentaries that are loaded with orthodoxy or read them carefully with the full knowledge that they promote man-made doctrines which may be opposed by God's Word. Ergo, read the Word, not man's thoughts of what the Word may or may not say.

First Two Lessons From God's Word

The first two lessons in this book from God's Word are from Jesus Christ:

1. Many Church authorities and leaders are mistaken and do not know Scripture or the power of God. This means you cannot rely solely upon the Church and its leaders for truth concerning God's Word.
2. We must live by every word that proceeds out of the mouth of God. This means we must know God's Word if we truly seek the truth.

Church Tradition Negates God's Commandments

> "[Jesus] answered and said to them [the Church leaders at that time], 'Why do you also transgress the commandment of God because of your tradition?'" Matthew 15:3 (NKJV)

Trinity Dogma © 2009 Rev. Edward G. Palmer

> "[Jesus] answering, said to them: 'Why do you also transgress [and thereby negate the effect of] the commandment of God for [or by] your tradition?' " Matthew 15:3 (Douay-Rheims)

Would the Church and its leaders teach against God's Word? Negate HIS commandments by their own man-made "Church" traditions? The answer is yes, they would. And, I might add that it is not I, but our Lord Jesus Christ that makes this very clear. Even …

God HIMSELF weighs in on the issue of corrupting HIS Word in the book of Malachi.

> "For the lips of a priest should keep knowledge, and people should seek the law from his mouth; for he is the messenger of the LORD of hosts. But you have departed from the way; you have caused many to stumble at the law. You have corrupted the covenant of Levi," Says the LORD of hosts. "Therefore I also have made you contemptible and base before all the people, because you have not kept MY ways but have shown partiality in the law." Malachi 2:7-9 (NKJV)

> "For the lips of the priest shall keep knowledge, and they shall seek the law at his mouth: because he is the angel of the LORD of hosts. But you have departed out of the way, and have caused many to stumble at the law: you have made void the covenant of Levi, saith the LORD of hosts. Therefore have I also made you contemptible, and base before all people, as you have not kept my ways, and have accepted persons in the law." Malachi 2:7-9 (Douay-Rheims)

Third Lesson From God's Word

This lesson comes from both God HIMSELF and Jesus Christ HIS begotten human Son.

   3. The Church will negate God's commandments through their man-made traditions.

Jesus gives us a clear illustration in Matthew of just how a man-made tradition negates God's commandments. So, let's go deeper into the teaching of Jesus at Matthew 15:3.

> [Jesus said:] "Why do you also transgress [negate] the commandment of God because of your tradition? For God commanded, saying, 'Honor your father and your mother'; and, 'He who curses father or mother, let him be put to death.' But you say, 'Whoever says to his father or mother, "Whatever profit you might have received from me is a gift to God" [meaning in this case, a gift to the church] -- then he need not honor his father or mother.'

> Thus you have made the commandment of God of no effect by your tradition. Hypocrites! Well did Isaiah prophesy about you, Saying:
>
> 'These people draw near to [God] with their mouth,
> And honor [God] with their lips,
> But their heart is far from [God].
> And in vain they worship [God],
> Teaching as doctrines the commandments of men.' "
>
> Matthew 15:3-9 (NKJV)

What caused people to worship God in vain? It was the teaching of man-made doctrines as commandments of God. That is exactly what the trinity doctrine is. It is a man-made doctrine that results in people worshipping God in vain. It's because, in reality, they are not worshipping God. In the trinity doctrine, they do not even know God and are literally wasting their time in idolatrous worship services. Ergo, they "worship God in vain." God especially does not listen to idolatrous Jesus worship. Worship of Jesus is an insult to the God who offered Jesus as a human sacrifice for our sins. It is an insult also to Jesus for the human sacrifice he made on our behalf. Who exactly did Jesus teach us to worship? The answer is in Matthew and it's plain for all to see. The phrase "the LORD your [thy] God" refers to the God Jesus serves and worships. It is Yahweh, the God of the Jews.

> Then Jesus said to him, "Away with you, Satan! For it is written, 'You shall worship the LORD your God, and HIM only you shall serve.' "
>
> Matthew 4:10 (NKJV)

> Then Jesus saith to him: "Begone, Satan: for it is written, The LORD thy God shalt thou adore, and HIM only shalt thou serve."
>
> Matthew 4:10 (Douay-Rheims)

Jesus confirms his identity as "the Son of Man" and as "Christ, the Son of the living God" to Peter in this exchange of words:

> "When Jesus came into the region of Caesarea Philippi, he asked his disciples, saying, 'who do men say that I, the Son of Man, am?' So they said, 'Some say John the Baptist, some Elijah, and others Jeremiah or one of the prophets.' He said to them, 'But who do you say that I am?' Simon Peter answered and said, 'You are the Christ, the Son of the living God.' Jesus answered and said to him, 'Blessed are you, Simon Bar-Jonah, for flesh and blood has not revealed this to you, but my FATHER who is in Heaven. And I also say to you that you are Peter, and on this rock I will build my church, and the gates of Hades shall not prevail against it. And I will give you the keys of the kingdom of Heaven, and whatever you bind on earth will be bound in Heaven, and whatever you loose on earth will be loosed in Heaven.' "
>
> Matthew 16:13-18 (NKJV)

Jesus confirms the identity of his God and our God as "the FATHER."

> **Jesus said to her, "Do not cling to me, for I have not yet ascended to my FATHER; but go to my brethren and say to them, 'I am ascending to my FATHER and your FATHER, and to my God and your God.' "**
> **John 20:17 (NKJV)**

> **Jesus saith to her: "Do not touch me, for I am not yet ascended to my FATHER. But go to my brethren, and say to them: 'I ascend to my FATHER and to your FATHER, to my God and your God.' "**
> **John 20:17 (Douay-Rheims)**

> **Jesus said to her, "Stop holding on to me, for I have not yet ascended to the FATHER. But go to my brothers and tell them, 'I am going to my FATHER and your FATHER, to my God and your God.' "**
> **John 20:17 (NAB)** *New American Bible*

The *New American Bible* is the modern version of the Catholic *Douay-Rheims Bible*. You can see that nothing has changed in whom Jesus identifies as his God. The God that Jesus served and worshipped is the same God his Jewish forefathers served and worshipped. Jesus' God is called YAH, Yahweh, Jehovah or Yehovah. All four names refer to the same God worshipped by the Jews. We can see the name of God, YAH, is fully disclosed in the Old Testament in some translations. The word Hallelujah is derived directly from the Hebrew language and means to "praise ye the LORD" or more simply "praise Yahweh!"

> "Sing to God, sing praises to HIS name; Extol HIM who rides on the clouds, By HIS name YAH, And rejoice before HIM." Psalms 68:4 (NKJV)

> "Behold, God is my salvation, I will trust and not be afraid; 'For YAH, the LORD, is my strength and song; HE also has become my salvation.' "
> Isaiah 12:2 (NKJV)

> "Trust in the LORD forever, For in YAH, the LORD, [God Almighty] is [our] everlasting strength." Isaiah 26:4 (NKJV)

---

hallelujah : ˌhaləˈlooyə: (also **alleluia**)

Noun — an utterance of the word "hallelujah" as an expression of worship or rejoicing.

ORIGIN Old English, via ecclesiastical Latin **alleluia** from Greek **allēlouia** (in the Septuagint), or (from the 16th century) directly from Hebrew **hallĕlūyāh** *'praise ye the LORD.'*

New Oxford American Dictionary, Apple OSX Dictionary Version 2.0.2 (51.4)

The FATHER is the God identified in the New Testament!

Trinity Dogma © 2009 Rev. Edward G. Palmer

To Claim Jesus Is God Makes Jesus A Liar!
Such A The Claim Repudiates Jesus' Actual Teachings!

No Christian will be able to stand before God and say that he did not know the name of the ONE and "only true God." Jesus simplified God's name for us by teaching us to call God, the FATHER! When anyone claims that Jesus is God, it is a direct repudiation of the teachings of Jesus about his God. In other words, to call Jesus God, literally makes Jesus a liar in light of Jesus' New Testament teachings. Listen to more of what Jesus taught.

> **Jesus said to the FATHER: "And this is eternal life, that they may know YOU, the only true God, and Jesus Christ whom YOU have sent." John 17:3 (NKJV)**

> **Jesus said to the FATHER: "Now this is everlasting life, that they may know THEE, the only true God, and him whom thou hast sent, Jesus Christ." John 17:3 (Douay-Rheims)**

> **Jesus said to the FATHER: "Now this is eternal life, that they should know YOU, the only true God, and the one whom you sent, Jesus Christ." John 17:3 (NAB)**

If you do not know Yahweh, you certainly do not know Jesus! To know Jesus means you actually listen to his teachings and obey what he has commanded of us. Jesus continues on in John 17 and we read:

> **"Holy FATHER [my God], keep through YOUR name those whom YOU have given me, that they may be one as we are. While I was with them in the world, I kept them in YOUR name." John 17:11-12 (NKJV)**

> **"O righteous FATHER! The world has not known YOU, but I have known YOU; and these have known that YOU sent me. And I have declared to them YOUR name, and will declare it, that the love with which YOU loved me may be in them, and I in them."**
> **   John 17:25-26 (NKJV)**

Jesus Declared God's Name To Us!

My spirit has felt very grieved writing the prior three pages. Grief and sorrow have descended upon my heart and my eyes have welled up with tears. I can sense my spirit crying out to God: "Have mercy on Christians FATHER!" Why? It's because the words of my brother and Lord, Jesus Christ, are now of so little value in Christianity. It's because so many Christians now worship Jesus instead of the God that Jesus taught us to worship. Indeed my eyes ache and my head pounds in sorrow and I wonder why I am being asked by God to write these words. I even lament, FATHER, what good are all these words?

Mythology and man-made doctrines have clouded and distorted God's Holy Word and the teachings of HIS only human begotten Son, Jesus Christ. Indeed, have mercy O' God on all the confused Christians who now live in error and have substituted your Son as their god to be worshipped. You see, God interrupted me and had me place the above Scriptures in front of you. My hands surrendered to HIS will and it is no longer I at this keyboard, but the Spirit of HIM working through me, once again, WHO wants you to know the truth of HIS Word. How, when Jesus has fully taught us about his ONE "and only true God," [Yahweh], can any claim that Jesus himself is God? Yet, I know there is so much more. Even now God's Spirit says to consider these verses on whom to worship.

> "And I fell down before his feet to worship him [the angel]. And he said to me, 'Thou must not do that. I am a fellow servant of thine and of thy brethren who give the testimony of Jesus. <u>Worship God!</u> For the testimony of Jesus is the spirit of prophecy.'"
> **Revelation 19:10 (Douay-Rheims)**

> "And I, John, am he who heard and saw these things. And when I heard and saw, I fell down to worship at the feet of the angel who showed me these things. And he said to me, 'Thou must not do that. I am a fellow servant of thine and of thy brethren the prophets, and of those who keep the words of this book. <u>Worship God!</u>"
> **Revelation 22:8-9 (Douay-Rheims)**

Worship God, who Jesus identified as the FATHER!

> Jesus said: "He who overcomes, I will make him a pillar in the temple of <u>my God</u>, and never more shall he go outside. And I will write upon him the name of <u>my God</u>, and the name of the city of <u>my God</u>—the new Jerusalem, which comes down out of Heaven from <u>my God</u>—and my new name." Revelation 3:12 (Douay-Rheims)

Jesus said:

- Temple of <u>my God</u>
- Name of <u>my God</u>
- City of <u>my God</u>
- City comes out of Heaven from <u>my God</u>

Ergo, Jesus taught us about *his* God, whose name is Yahweh. Jesus did not teach us that he was God. The Church trinity dogma teaches that Jesus is God. The trinity is NOT the "only true God" Jesus taught us about. Jesus taught us to call God our heavenly FATHER. He taught us to worship only *his* God. And, while it is true that some people worshipped Jesus in the Bible, it is just as true that Jesus did not teach us to worship him! And, make a note: people also worshipped Paul and Barnabas in the Bible. Jesus also taught us to honor him. We do this every time we pray to the FATHER in Jesus' name. We do this also when we obey Jesus' teachings. Do you obey Jesus' teaching in Matthew 4:10?

Jesus also gave us some other information about who he was. Consider for example Revelation 3:14 and Colossians 1:15 in the Catholic Douay-Rheims Bible.

> **Jesus said: "These things says the Amen, the Faithful and True Witness, the Beginning of the creation of God." Rev 3:14 (NKJV)**
>
> **Jesus said: "Thus says the Amen, the faithful and true witness, <u>who</u> is the beginning of the creation of God." Revelation 3:14 (Douay-Rheims)**
>
> **"He [Christ] is the image of the invisible God, the firstborn over all creation." Colossians 1:15 (NKJV)**
>
> **"He [Christ] is the image of the invisible God, the firstborn of every creature." Colossians 1:15 (Douay-Rheims)**
>
> **"He [Christ] is the image of the invisible God, the firstborn of all creation." Colossians 1:15 (NRSV)**

The above two verses in Revelation 3:14 and Colossians 1:15 were altered in some bibles to support orthodox theology which teaches Jesus is God. The Catholic *Douay-Rheims Bible* translation of Revelation 3:14 best states the identity of Christ. In this version, Christ was God's first creation. Ergo, God created the angel Christ and then used Christ in the rest of His creation. Some believe Christ is an angel who is called "Immanuel."

Christ says <u>he</u> was God's first creation, the beginning!

Some translations alter the above verses to read that Christ was "at the beginning" of God's creation implying Christ was always eternal. This is not what the Bible teaches. It is man-made doctrine. So, if Christ was an angel God created first and who was then used in the creation of this world and of man, is there more Scripture support? There should be little disagreement Christ was used by God in His creative works. However, consider Hebrews chapter 1 in regards to Christ, an angel elevated by God to be "His Son."

> **"God, who, at sundry times and in divers manners, spoke in times past to the fathers by the prophets, last of all, in these days hath spoken to us by His Son [Jesus Christ], whom He hath appointed heir of all things, by whom also He made the world. Who [Jesus Christ] being the brightness of His glory, and the figure of His substance, and upholding all things by the Word of His power, making purgation of sins, sitteth on the right hand of the Majesty on high."**
>
> **<u>"Being made so much better than the [other] angels</u>, as he [Jesus] hath inherited a more excellent name than they [the other angels]. <u>For to which of the [other] angels hath He [God] said</u> at any time, Thou art My Son, to day have I begotten [made] thee? And again, I will be to him [Jesus] a Father, and he shall be to Me a Son? "**

Trinity Dogma © 2009 Rev. Edward G. Palmer

> "And again, when HE [God] bringeth in the first begotten [Christ, the first creation of God] into the world, HE saith: And let all the [other] angels of God adore him [Jesus Christ]."
> **Hebrews 1:1-6 (Douay-Rheims)**

> "Thou [Christ] hast loved justice and hated iniquity; therefore God, thy God, has anointed thee with the oil of gladness <u>above thy fellows</u>."
> **Hebrews 1:9 (Douay-Rheims)**

> "You [Jesus] have loved righteousness and hated wickedness; therefore God, your God, has anointed you [Jesus] with the oil of gladness <u>beyond your companions</u> [other angels Jesus fellowshipped with in Heaven]." **Hebrews 1:9 (NRSV)**

Hebrews 1:7-8 is left out intentionally as these verses are esoteric in nature and are among a handful of verses that contradict the teachings of Jesus. As such, they must be deemed as errant. Therefore, I choose to believe the teachings of Jesus over the handful of verses that contradict his words. As of this date, the author of the book of Hebrews is also unknown. Ergo, no weight can be given to words that contradict Jesus' teachings.

Now think about this particular verse in the Douay-Rheims Bible to illustrate exactly what I am talking about here when it comes to textually errant bible verses.

> "Looking for the blessed hope and glorious coming of our great God and Savior, Jesus Christ, who gave himself for us that he might redeem us from all iniquity and cleanse for himself an acceptable people, pursuing good works." **Titus 2:13-14 (Douay-Rheims)**

From a textual analysis, something must be wrong in the above verse even if someone I love considers it trustworthy. It isn't! Some scribe had his hand at work and altered this version of the verse. We have already seen in this same Bible where Jesus states that the FATHER is God. We have also seen in this same Bible where Jesus states it is he who was created first by God. Yet in this verse, it distinctly states that Jesus Christ is our great God and Savior. Someone decided to alter the meaning of the text by the insertion of a simple comma. Consider the meaning of these two lines, one with a comma deleted.

[The] coming of our great God and Savior, Jesus Christ. (One entity is coming)

[The] coming of our great God <u>and</u> Savior Jesus Christ. (Two entities coming)

Some may argue they have the same meaning, but it is clear that one states Jesus is God in spite of what Jesus taught us about who God was. In one verse there is one entity coming back. In the second meaning there are two entities coming back. You should be aware that the Bible teaches us that two entities are coming back. We are taught in Scripture that Jesus comes back. We are also taught in Scripture that God HIMSELF comes back. Ergo, some scribe added a comma so the verse would support the trinity dogma even if it contradicts other verses in the same Bible. Who will you believe? Jesus?

Trinity Dogma © 2009 Rev. Edward G. Palmer

Your Bible study can take you deeper down this textual criticism and analysis by simply looking at other translations of the same verse, Titus 2:13-14. For convenience, here are a few other translations to compare against the Douay-Rheims version.

> **"As we await the blessed hope, the appearance of the glory of the great God and of our savior Jesus Christ." NAB (New American Bible)**

The NAB is the current authorized Catholic Bible, which fixes the earlier error.

> **"Looking for the blessed hope and glorious appearing of our great God and Savior Jesus Christ." NKJV**

> **"While we wait for the blessed hope and the manifestation of the glory of our great God and Savior, Jesus Christ." NRSV**

> **"Waiting in hope for the blessing which will come with the appearing of the glory of our great God and Saviour Christ Jesus." NJB (New Jerusalem)**

All who believe that Jesus is God will be quite surprised when Jesus and Yahweh both show up. Most newer translations fix the error found in the older Douay-Rheims verse, but not all. The fact that there are such nuances in various versions of the Bible should not discourage you from reading the Bible. I believe all bibles are over 98% in agreement with each other. You will need three bibles to safely study Scripture. The errors like the one above will show themselves untrue with multiple bibles. In addition, the more you know about God's Word, the more these types of errors will become self evident to you. Before you study the Bible ask God to give you wisdom and He will.

Now, before proceeding, who was it that Apostle Paul claimed is God? We see Paul's answer in 1 Corinthians 8:3-6 as follows:

> **"But if anyone loves God, this one is known by Him. Therefore concerning the eating of things offered to idols, we know that an idol is nothing in the world, and <u>that there is no other God but one</u>. For even if there are so-called gods, whether in Heaven or on earth (as there are many gods and many lords), <u>yet for us there is one God, the Father</u>, of whom are all things, and we for Him; and one Lord Jesus Christ, through whom are all things, and through whom we live." 1 Corinthians 8:3-6 (NKJV)**

> **"But if any love God, the same is known by Him. But as for the meats that are sacrificed to idols, we know that an idol is nothing in the world, and that <u>there is no God but one</u>. For although there be that are called gods, either in Heaven or on earth (for there be gods many, and lords many); <u>Yet to us there is but one God, the Father</u>, of whom are all things, and we unto Him; and one Lord Jesus Christ, by whom are all things, and we by him."**
> **1 Corinthians 8:3-6 (Douay-Rheims)**

Apostle Paul taught:

1. **There is one God, the FATHER**
2. **All things are of the FATHER**
3. **There is one Lord Jesus Christ**
4. **All things are through our Lord Jesus Christ**

> *We live for God **through** the strength and help of both Christ's Spirit and God's Spirit. Ergo, both Christ and God HIMSELF will dwell inside the hearts of all true believers.*

Jesus said: "If anyone loves me [Jesus], he will keep my word; and my FATHER [God] will love him, and we [Jesus and his God] will come to him and make our home with him." John 14:23 (NKJV)

In Jesus own words, we can understand that there will only be one God inside of us, but two of God's servants. Those two servants will be the Spirit of Christ and the Holy Spirit or "Spirit of Truth." We see Jesus confirming that God HIMSELF will send HIS Holy Spirit to us. Note: This is *not* "God the Holy Spirit" as so many Christians claim. It is the "Holy Spirit" or "Spirit of Truth" sent by the FATHER."

Jesus said: "I will ask the FATHER, and HE shall give you another Paraclete, that HE may abide with you for ever. The spirit of truth, whom the world cannot receive, because it seeth him not, nor knoweth him: but you shall know him; because he shall abide with you, and shall be in you." John 14:16-17 (Douay-Rheims)

Jesus said: "But the Paraclete, the Holy Ghost, whom the FATHER will send in my name, he will teach you all things, and bring all things to your mind, whatsoever I shall have said to you."
John 14:26 (Douay-Rheims)

In the above verses in John, we see that the Paraclete is identified as both the Spirit of Truth and the Holy Spirit. This should not be confused with the Spirit of Holiness. Note: All seven of the Spirits of God have been previously identified in the message titled: "*The Seven Spirits*." So we can see both God Almighty along with HIS Son Christ dwelling within us through the Holy Spirit God has sent to us who are true believers. Jesus teaches that this Spirit will "teach you all things" and bring back to your mind "whatever [Jesus] [has] said to [us]" [John 14:26]. We also see that God sends HIS Holy Spirit to us so "that HE HIMSELF may abide with us for ever" [John 14:16-17].

God uses HIS Holy Spirit to communicate with us!

Trinity Dogma © 2009 Rev. Edward G. Palmer

Antichrist Spirit Teaches Against Christ's Humanity

"Dearly beloved, believe not every spirit, but try the spirits if they be of God: because many false prophets are gone out into the world. By this is the spirit of God known. Every spirit which confesseth that Jesus Christ is come in the flesh, is of God: And every spirit that dissolveth Jesus, is not of God: and this is Antichrist, of whom you have heard that he cometh, and he is now already in the world."
1 John 4:1-3 (Douay-Rheims)

"Beloved, do not believe every spirit, but test the spirits, whether they are of God; because many false prophets have gone out into the world. By this you know the Spirit of God: Every spirit that confesses that Jesus Christ has come in the flesh is of God, and every spirit that does not confess that Jesus Christ has come in the flesh is not of God. And this is the spirit of the Antichrist, which you have heard was coming, and is now already in the world." 1 John 4:1-3 (NKJV)

"Beloved, do not trust every spirit but test the spirits to see whether they belong to God, because many false prophets have gone out into the world. This is how you can know the Spirit of God: every spirit that acknowledges Jesus Christ [has] come in the flesh belongs to God, and every spirit that does not acknowledge Jesus [in the flesh] does not belong to God. This is the spirit of the antichrist that, as you heard, is to come, but in fact is already in the world."
1 John 4:1-3 (NAB)

Nine Antichrist Teachings

1. The antichrist teaches against the 100% humanity of Jesus Christ.
2. The antichrist teaches Christ was 100% man and 100% God to confuse people.
3. The antichrist teaches it was God who came down to die for your sins on a cross.
4. The antichrist teaches you can't help yourself and cannot be a righteous human.
5. The antichrist teaches that Christ is "God the FATHER."
6. The antichrist teaches that Mary is "Mother of God."
7. The antichrist teaches that the Holy Spirit from God is "God the Holy Spirit."
8. The antichrist teaches that Jesus is "God the Son."
9. The antichrist teaches that Jesus was not made, that he was eternal.

"Wherefore it behoved him [Jesus] in all things to be **made** like unto his brethren, that he might become a merciful and faithful priest before God, that he might be a propitiation for the sins of the people." Hebrews 2:17 (Douay-Rheims)

Trinity Dogma © 2009 Rev. Edward G. Palmer

"Therefore, he [Jesus] had to <u>become like his brothers in every way</u>, that he might be a merciful and faithful high priest before God to expiate the sins of the people." Hebrews 2:17 (NAB)

"Therefore, in all things he [Jesus] had to be **made** like his brethren, that he might be a merciful and faithful High Priest in things pertaining to God, to make propitiation for the sins of the people." Hebrews 2:17 (NKJV)

"But not as the offence, so also the gift. For if by the offence of one, many died; much more the grace of God, and the gift, by the grace of <u>**one man, Jesus Christ**</u>, hath abounded unto many."
                                                                Romans 5:15 (Douay-Rheims)

"But the free gift is not like the offense. For if by the one man's offense many died, much more the grace of God and the gift by the **grace of the <u>one Man, Jesus Christ</u>**, abounded to many." Romans 5:15 (NKJV)

"But the gift is not like the transgression. For if by that one person's transgression the many died, how much more did the grace of God and the gracious **gift of the <u>one person Jesus Christ</u>** overflow for the many." Romans 5:15 (NAB)

Prayer*: Father God, I pray that You will bind every spirit that speaks against the full humanity of Your only begotten human Son Jesus. He was fully a human like every other human that ever existed. To experience our humanity, You sent Christ to become incarnate as a man. Yet, in spite of Jesus' faithful teachings and service to You, the Antichrist has established a stronghold in the minds of over 90% of those who claim to be a Christian. These people are programmed by the Church trinity dogma, are woefully ignorant of Scripture and they need Your help in opening up their minds and hearts. Therefore, I also pray that You will loose the minds of all who have a sincere heart and who desire to be true followers of Jesus Christ. Only by recognizing Jesus as a human and the trinity doctrine as a false dogma of the Church can their minds be freed. Father, in these End-Times, free Your people to acknowledge Jesus Christ was only human and that at no point was he ever our God. Help them to understand that Jesus was another messenger You sent and that as a human, Christ brought us Your Word so we could more fully understand You. And, that Jesus now serves as our high priest sitting at your right hand. Help them to understand that the Holy Spirit is a gift from You and has no throne besides You and Christ, but is an active servant of Yours on earth to teach us what You need us to know. Therefore Father, I pray that You will bind all spirits from interfering with the people's understanding of these words. Finally, I pray you will loose every mind that reads these words to fully understand Your Scripture. Edward*

Jesus was <u>MADE</u> a <u>MAN</u> and human like <u>ALL</u> humans!

| **Lessons Four Through Thirty-Eight** |

4. People worship God in vain as a direct result of Church teachings and traditions.
5. Jesus taught us to "worship only the LORD your [our] God!"
6. Jesus was worshipped in the New Testament, but never taught us to worship him.
7. Paul and Barnabas were also worshipped in the New Testament.
8. Jesus confirms his identity to Peter as the "Son of Man" and also as the "Son of the living God." Note: "Son of living God" <u>does not mean</u> he is "God the Son."
9. Jesus states that the FATHER [God] revealed who Jesus was to Peter.

   Pray that the FATHER [God] will also reveal Jesus to you. And while you are at it, pray that Jesus will reveal the FATHER to you.

   "All things are delivered to me [Jesus] by my FATHER [God]. And no one knoweth the Son, but the FATHER: <u>neither doth any one know the FATHER, but the Son</u>, and he [or she] to whom it shall please the Son [Jesus] to <u>reveal HIM</u> [God]." Matthew 11:27 (Douay-Rheims)

10. Jesus taught us that the FATHER was his God and also our God.
11. Jesus identified who God was in the New Testament. God is the FATHER!
12. Apostle Paul taught us that the FATHER was his God and also our God.
13. Apostle Paul identified who God was in the New Testament. God is the FATHER!
14. God's name is identified in some translations as Yah.
15. The God Jesus worshipped and served was the God his ancestors worshipped and served. *It was the God of the Jews who was known as Yah, Yahweh, Jehovah and Yehovah who is identified in Jewish Scripture as YWHW, the Tetragrammaton.*
16. There is only ONE God defined in the New Testament [and it is not Jesus].
17. Eternal life comes from knowing who God really is and in knowing who Christ is.
18. Jesus kept his disciples in God's name, not in his own name.
19. Jesus always declared his God to his disciples. Jesus did not teach a trinity dogma.
20. God's Word teaches us to worship only HIM and not to worship Jesus.
21. Jesus used the words "my God" multiple times in Scripture in referring to God.
22. Jesus taught that he himself was the first act of God's creation. Ergo, Jesus was the "beginning of the creative works of God" or "God's first creation."
23. Jesus is identified as "the image of God" and "the firstborn of all creation."
24. God elevated Jesus higher than all other angels and called Jesus "MY Son."

25. A handful of verses in various translations have been modified to support the trinity dogma, but speak directly against the teachings of Jesus Christ.
26. The Bible teaches that both Jesus and his God will come back to be with us.
27. You cannot create a doctrine or teaching that negates the Word of God.
28. You cannot create a doctrine or teaching that negates the teachings of Christ.
29. The trinity doctrine negates both the word of God and the teachings of Christ.
30. Paul teaches we are all of God, but that we live for God through Jesus Christ.
31. God uses His Holy Spirit to speak directly to us thereby dwelling within us.
32. God uses His Holy Spirit to remind us of what Christ taught.
33. In reminding us of Christ's teachings, the Spirit of Christ also dwells within us.
34. Make a note. The Holy Spirit speaks to us for God and about Christ, His Son.
35. The Antichrist speaks against the full humanity of Jesus in a variety of ways.
36. Jesus was MADE exactly like all other human beings.
37. Jesus was made a MALE HUMAN in every respect just like other human males.
38. Jesus was born from a FEMALE HUMAN who was also human in every respect.

"God is <u>Not</u> a Man" — "<u>Nor</u> as the <u>Son of Man</u>!"

"<u>God is not a man</u>, that He should lie, <u>nor as the son of man</u>, <u>that He should be changed</u>. Hath He said then, and will He not do? Hath He spoken, and will He not fulfill?" Numbers 23:19 (Douay-Rheims)

"<u>God is not man</u> that He should speak falsely, <u>nor human</u>, that He should change his mind. Is He one to speak and not act, to decree and not fulfill?" Numbers 23:19 (NAB)

"<u>God is not a man</u>, that He should lie, <u>nor a son of man</u>, that He should repent. Has He said, and will He not do? Or has He spoken, and will He not make it good?" Numbers 23:19 (NKJV)

Here within two well-respected Catholic Bibles, the *Douay-Rheims* and the *New American Bible* there is a direct contradiction to the Church trinity dogma, which declares Jesus "God the Son." Perk up your ears, especially if you are Catholic. Listen, I suspect many of you have ignored all of the Scriptures and Bible lessons God has given you in the preceding pages. Ignore them at your own eternal peril. Consider that both of these Catholic bibles have Jesus declaring he is the "Son of Man" and has Paul teaching that Jesus was indeed a "Man." Now, explain to this apostle how anyone can reconcile the Church trinity dogma with those teachings and the above teaching in the same Catholic bibles that teach God was neither a "Son of Man" nor was He a "human."

We know that we are all created in the image of God. We also know that God has given us the power of a strong mind [2 Timothy 1:7 NKJV]. Have you received a strong mind from God? You should be able to think through things both logically and spiritually if you have truly accepted Christ Jesus into your heart and returned back to God Almighty! And, isn't it God HIMSELF who dwells within you and I, as true believers, through HIS Holy Spirit? Making us of one mind with HIM? And, doesn't HIS Holy Spirit also remind us all of what Christ has taught us? So, given all of these Scriptural facts, why should anyone with a brain accept the trinity dogma? The answer is people have bought the trinity dogma on faith in their Church and through ignorance of God's Holy Word.

The trinity dogma cannot be justified given all of the Scripture presented in this book. It cannot be justified given the teachings of Jesus Christ about who he was and who his God was. And, given modern Bible software, anyone can see for them self the lie that the Church has perpetrated since 325 AD by studying God's Word. If you think back to 325 AD, you will realize that no bibles existed and all teachings were derived from hand written manuscripts. With only a few people having any authoritative Scripture in their possession, it was easy enough to program the people with any message the Church desired. Who could object? Guess I'm ranting in this paragraph. Please excuse me, but at least one inquiring mind wants to know. Write me with your rationale for how the above Scriptures can be so easily dismissed in favor of the Church tradition called the trinity.

I will give credit to the Douay-Rheims Catholic Bible for giving us the best translation of Numbers 23:19 from a spiritual standpoint. It states simply: "God is not a man." It states simply: "Nor as the Son of Man that HE should be changed." Jesus was a man, a fully 100% human male. Jesus taught us that he was the "Son of Man." And, we know that as the "Son of Man" Jesus was indeed changed and given a resurrection body. We also know that God elevated Jesus higher than the other angels because he was "begotten" as a human "Son of Man" and now carries the distinction of being God's *only begotten* human Son. Do you realize that Jesus Christ was not God's only son? If you believe this, you have been misled or remain woefully ignorant of Scripture. There are "sons of God." Yet, Jesus Christ is the only one that was begotten by God. Ergo, Jesus is the "Son of Man" or God's begotten Son; now elevated to a higher status than all the other angels of God.

Sons of God

"Blessed are the peacemakers, for they shall be called **sons of God**." Matthew 5:9 NKJV
(Douay-Rheims "children of God.")

"Nor can they die anymore, for they are equal to the angels and are **sons of God**, being Sons of the resurrection." Luke 20:36 NKJV (Douay-Rheims **sons of God**.)

"For as many as are led by the Spirit of God, these are sons of God." Romans 8:14 NKJV
(Douay-Rheims **sons of God**.)

"For the earnest expectation of the creation eagerly waits for the revealing of the **sons of God**." Romans 8:19 NKJV (Douay-Rheims **sons of God**.)

Trinity Dogma © 2009 Rev. Edward G. Palmer

"For you are all **sons of God** through faith in Christ Jesus." Galatians 3:26 NKJV
(Douay-Rheims "children of God.")

Many sons of God, <u>but</u> only one Begotten Son!

In the twisted logic of the Catholic Church, Mary becomes the "Mother of God." Yet, why wouldn't that make me and every other true believer "God the Son" or "God the Daughter?" And, why wouldn't it make every other mother who does the will of God the "Mother of God?" The same perverse logic would apply using simply the words of our Lord Jesus Christ. Listen carefully to Jesus' teaching about who is his brother, sister and mother.

> **Jesus said: "Behold my mother and my brethren. For whosoever shall do the will of my FATHER, that is in Heaven, he is my brother, and sister, and mother." Matthew 12:49-50 (Douay-Rheims)**

> **Jesus said: "Here are my mother and my brothers. For whoever does the will of my heavenly FATHER is my brother, and sister, and mother." Matthew 12:49-50 (NAB)**

In the perspective of Jesus, he had more than one mother. Virtually every mother that does the will of the FATHER in Heaven [God] is considered the mother of Jesus. I did not say it, Jesus Christ taught it! Likewise every woman or man who does the will of the FATHER in Heaven [God] is considered a brother or sister of Jesus Christ. Ergo, the phrase "Mary Mother of God" is without merit when viewed against the teachings of Christ.

Likewise, I myself am a brother of Christ since I do the will of our FATHER in Heaven. Using the perverted Church logic, since I am the brother of Jesus, that would make Mary my mother and also make me "God the Son." Of course, this is the perverted logic of New Age thinkers just taking the perverted Church logic to its next logical conclusion. Ergo, if Jesus is "God the Son" and if I am his brother, I am also "God the Son." If this discussion offends you, it should. Now, doesn't the Church logic, which is equally perverted in the light of Scripture, also offend you? The terms "Mary, Mother of God"; "God the Son"; and "God the Holy Spirit" are all offensive to the one true God Jesus taught us about. And, they are offensive because they cause people to commit idolatry.

As a servant of God, I am also HIS son. I am also the brother of our Lord Jesus Christ, who is our *head* apostle and high priest in Heaven and whose example I will follow to my own death as I seek to be faithful to God. Yet, can anyone be faithful, as Christ has commanded us when they believe a trinity doctrine that misleads people about who God is and about what HIS true nature is?

Jesus, God's Apostle And High Priest

"Wherefore, holy brethren, partakers of the heavenly vocation, <u>consider the apostle and high priest of our confession, Jesus</u>: Who is faithful to HIM <u>that made him</u>, as was also Moses in all his house."
Hebrews 3:1-2 (Douay-Rheims)

Jesus, God's Prophet

A: God's plan to raise up a prophet

Moses said: "The LORD thy God will raise up to thee a prophet of thy nation and of thy brethren like unto me: him thou shalt hear: As thou desiredst of the LORD thy God in Horeb, when the assembly was gathered together, and saidst: Let me not hear any more the voice of the LORD my God, neither let me see any more this exceeding great fire, lest I die. And the LORD said to me: They have spoken all things well. I will raise them up a prophet out of the midst of their brethren like to thee: and I will put MY words in his mouth, and he shall speak to them all that I shall command him."
Deuteronomy 18:15-18 (Douay-Rheims)

Moses said: "A prophet like me will the LORD, your God, raise up for you from among your own kinsmen; to him you shall listen. This is exactly what you requested of the LORD, your God, at Horeb on the day of the assembly, when you said, 'Let us not again hear the voice of the LORD, our God, nor see this great fire any more, lest we die.' And the LORD said to me, 'this was well said. I will raise up for them a prophet like you from among their kinsmen, and will put MY words into his mouth; he shall tell them all that I command him."
Deuteronomy 18:15-18 (NAB)

B. How to recognize a prophet

Moses said: "If you say to yourselves, 'How can we recognize an oracle [Word] which the LORD has spoken?' know that, even though a prophet speaks in the name of the LORD, if his oracle [word] is not fulfilled or verified, it is an oracle [word] which the LORD did not speak. The prophet has spoken it presumptuously, and you shall have no fear of him." Deuteronomy 18:22 (Douay-Rheims)

C. False prophets are slain

God said: "But the prophet, who being corrupted with pride, shall speak in MY name things that I did not command him to say, or in the name of strange gods, shall be slain." Deut. 18:20 (Douay-Rheims)

D: Jesus declares he is a prophet

"But Jesus said to them: A prophet is not without honour, save in his own country, and in his own house." Matthew 13:57 (Douay-Rheims)

Jesus said to them, "A prophet is not without honor except in his native place and in his own house." Matthew 13:57 (NAB)

Trinity Dogma © 2009 Rev. Edward G. Palmer

E: <u>Jesus teachings were from God</u>

Jesus answered them, and said: "My doctrine is not mine, but HIS that sent me." John 7:16 (Douay-Rheims)

Jesus said: "My teaching is not my own but is from the ONE [God] who sent me." John 7:16 (Douay-Rheims)

F: <u>Jesus spoke what God told him to say</u>

Jesus said: "He that loveth me not, keepeth not my words. And the word, which you have heard, is not mine; but the FATHER'S [God] who sent me." John 14:24 (Douay-Rheims)

Jesus said: "Whoever does not love me does not keep my words; yet the word you hear is not mine but that of the FATHER [God] who sent me." John 14:24 (NAB)

Discussion: God has asked me to keep the focus on Catholic bibles in this book for the benefit of all Catholics. That's why the *Douay-Rheims* and *New American Bible* are the only ones shown above. I believe it is well accepted by the Church that the prophecy in Deuteronomy 18:15-18 pertains to Jesus Christ. In both Catholic bibles, Jesus declares that he is a prophet. In both bibles, Jesus indicates that his teachings and doctrines are received from God Almighty. Jesus states clearly in both bibles that it is God whom he speaks for and Jesus has taught us the FATHER is God. Furthermore, Jesus taught us that he did not do anything of his own accord, but only what the FATHER [God] told him and/or taught him to do. The phrase "HIM who sent me" is a direct reference by Jesus to his God. Again and again, Jesus identified his and our God as the FATHER!

> **Jesus said: "I came down from Heaven, not to do my own will, but the will of HIM that sent me." John 6:38 (Douay-Rheims)**
>
> **Jesus said: "I must work the works of HIM [God] that sent me, whilst it is day: the night cometh, when no man can work."**
> **John 9:4 (Douay-Rheims)**
>
> **Jesus said: "My meat [food] is to do the will of HIM that sent me, that I may perfect [finish] HIS work." John 4:34 (Douay-Rheims)**
>
> **Jesus said: "I cannot of myself do any thing. As I hear, so I judge: and my judgment is just, because I seek not my own will, but the will of HIM that sent me." John 5:30 (Douay-Rheims)**
>
> **God said: "Before I formed thee [Jeremiah] in the bowels of thy mother, I knew thee: and before thou camest forth out of the womb, I sanctified thee, and made thee a prophet unto the nations."**
> **Jeremiah 1:5 (Douay-Rheims)**

Side Note: Consider Jeremiah 1:5 and how wonderfully it also speaks of Jesus, the man.

Clearly Jesus fulfilled the role of prophet while on this earth and according to his own words, not mine. In this role, he spoke for God and not on his own accord. Therefore the Church in making Jesus "God the Son" perverts the teachings of Jesus and the role that God assigned to him. The ignorance of the typical parishioner when it comes to Scripture allows the trinity dogma to be perpetuated indefinitely in spite of the teachings of Jesus. In addition, every priest since 325 AD was "programmed" with the trinity dogma and forbidden to do anything but rationalize this false doctrine by ignoring God's Word.

Would you worship any apostle? Would you worship any priest? Would you worship the High Priest of God? What about a prophet? Would you worship him? If the answer is no to all of these questions, why do you still seek to worship Jesus? There is one thing you should do with a prophet of God. You should fear and respect him. It is clear that very few within Christianity fear the prophet Jesus. Their lack of respect is demonstrated by their refusal to acknowledge the God he taught us about and obey his other teachings. Those teachings, I might add, having been received directly from God. Ergo, Jesus <u>was</u> the Word manifested in the flesh to us. Likewise, every prophet in the Bible, who was a prophet of God, <u>was also</u> the Word manifested in the flesh. Then, there is the fact that Jesus was also manifested in the flesh, as the seed of David, just as God had promised.

Jesus, Seed of David - In The Flesh

"Concerning His Son [Jesus], who was made to him [Joseph] of the seed of David, <u>according to the flesh</u>." Romans 1:3 (Douay-Rheims)

Jesus, Son of God - In The Spirit

"[Jesus] was predestinated the Son of God in power, <u>according to the spirit</u> of sanctification." Romans 1:4 (Douay-Rheims)

Jesus, Angel Of God

Paul said: "You despised not, nor rejected: but received me as an angel of God, even as Christ Jesus." Galatians 4:14 (Douay-Rheims)

Jesus, Archangel Of God

"For the Lord [Jesus Christ] himself shall come down from Heaven with commandment, and with the voice of an archangel, and with the trumpet of God: and the dead who are in Christ, shall rise first."
                                              1 Thessalonians 4:15 (Douay-Rheims)

Jesus, Our Spiritual Rock

"For I would not have you ignorant, brethren, that our fathers were all under the cloud, and all passed through the sea. And all in Moses were baptized, in the cloud, and in the sea: And did all eat the same spiritual food, And all drank the same spiritual drink; (and they drank of the spiritual rock that followed them, and the rock was Christ.)" 1 Corinthians 10:1-4 (Douay-Rheims)

Don't Ask Of Jesus Christ Anymore; Go Directly To The FATHER!

"Angels" and "sons of God" are also discussed in Jude 1:6 [angels] and in Genesis 6:2-4 [sons of God]. In the context of these discussions, both have removed themselves from their heavenly habitation. They are both considered Elohim, or part of the family of God in Heaven. Ergo, they are heavenly beings. Elohim is an ancient term for heavenly beings and includes angels, sons of God and may also be used to describe God HIMSELF. El is an ancient term used for minor gods and may also be used to describe God HIMSELF.

It is clear that Scripture contains many descriptions of who Jesus was. Those descriptions include being "Son of God" and "Angel" and "Archangel." They point clearly to Christ being a heavenly being created first by God and then later descending "in spirit" and incarnate [flesh] as Jesus, the man, apostle, priest, and prophet of God. After Jesus was resurrected, God elevated him above all angels and he now sits at God's right hand. The Holy Spirit? Where does the Holy Spirit sit in relation to God's throne? Got an answer?

One of the last discussions Jesus had with his disciples contained instructions to not ask of him anything after his resurrection. Listen carefully to Jesus' instructions. For all who pray to Jesus or someone else instead of God Almighty [the Father], you need to change your prayer life. Jesus gave you the formula to get your prayers answered. Use it!

> **Jesus said: "And in that day you shall not ask me any thing. Amen, amen I say to you: if you ask the FATHER any thing in my name ... HE will give it you. Hitherto you have not asked any thing in my name. Ask, and you shall receive; that your joy may be full. These things I have spoken to you in proverbs. The hour cometh, when I will no more speak to you in proverbs, but will shew you plainly of the FATHER. In that day you shall ask in my name; and <u>I say not to you, that I will ask the FATHER for you</u>: For the FATHER himself loveth you, because you have loved me, and have believed that I came out from God. I came forth from the FATHER, and am come into the world: again I leave the world, and I go to the FATHER."**
> **John 16:23-28 (Douay-Rheims)**

Jesus said: "On that day you will not question [ask] me about anything. Amen, amen, I say to you, whatever you ask the FATHER in my name HE will give you. Until now you have not asked anything in my name; ask and you will receive, so that your joy may be complete. I have told you this in figures of speech. The hour is coming when I will no longer speak to you in figures but I will tell you clearly about the FATHER. On that day you will ask in my name, and <u>I do not tell you that I will ask the FATHER for you</u>. For the FATHER himself loves you, because you have loved me and have come to believe that I came from God. I came from the FATHER and have come into the world. Now I am leaving the world and going back to the FATHER."

John 16:23-28 (NAB)

Jesus said: "At that time [after Christ's resurrection] you won't need to ask me for anything, for you can go directly to the FATHER and ask HIM, and HE will give you what you ask for because you use my name. You haven't tried this before, but begin now. Ask, using my name, and you will receive, and your cup of joy will overflow. I have spoken of these matters very guardedly, but the time will come when this will not be necessary and I will tell you plainly all about the FATHER. Then you will present your petitions over my signature! And I won't need to ask the FATHER to grant you these requests, for <u>the FATHER HIMSELF loves you dearly because you love me and believe that I came from the FATHER</u>. Yes, I came from the FATHER into the world and will leave the world and return to the FATHER." John 16:23-28 (Living Bible)

Seven Teachings of Jesus

1. Jesus will no longer pray to the FATHER [God] for us.
2. Jesus tells us to pray directly to the FATHER [God] ourselves.
3. Jesus teaches us to pray to the FATHER in his name so we will receive.
4. Jesus teaches we won't need to ask of him, because we can go directly to God.
5. The FATHER loves you because in part you believe Jesus came from the FATHER.
6. Jesus came from the FATHER, which Jesus identified to us as his/our God.
7. Jesus returns to the FATHER, which Jesus identified to us as his/our God.

Take your prayers <u>directly</u> to the FATHER in Jesus' name,
If you want them answered! That's what Jesus taught!

"Who is he who overcomes the world, but he who believes that Jesus is the Son of God?" 1 John 5:5 (NKJV)

"Who is he that overcometh the world, but he that believeth that Jesus is the Son of God?" 1 John 5:5 (Douay-Rheims)

It <u>doesn't say believe in</u> "God the Son." To <u>overcome</u> this world,
You believe that Jesus is the "Son of God." There is a big difference!

Do Not Add or Subtract from God's Word

"What I command thee, that only do thou to the LORD: neither add any thing, nor diminish." Deuteronomy 12:32 (Douay-Rheims)

"Whatever I command you, be careful to observe it; you shall not add to it nor take away from it." Deuteronomy 12:32 (NKJV)

"Every command that I enjoin on you, you shall be careful to observe, neither adding to it nor subtracting from it." Deut. 12:32 (NAB)

"For I testify to every one that heareth the words of the prophecy of this book: If any man shall add to these things, God shall add unto him the plagues written in this book. And if any man shall take away from the words of the book of this prophecy, God shall take away his part out of the book of life, and out of the holy city, and from these things that are written in this book."
                                         Revelation 22:18-19 (Douay-Rheims)

Do not add, subtract or otherwise alter the meaning of God's Word!

Warning from the *Book of Enoch*

"Then I [Enoch] inquired of one of the holy angels who was with me, and said, what is this splendid object? For it is not Heaven, but a flame of fire, alone which blazes, and in it there is the clamor of exclamation, of woe, and of great suffering. He [the angel] said, There, into that place which thou beholdest, <u>shall be thrust the spirits</u> of sinners and blasphemers; of those who shall do evil, and <u>who shall pervert all which God has spoken by the mouth of the prophets</u>; all which they ought to do." Enoch (Book of Enoch CV: 22-23)

Woe to all who pervert the teachings of our Lord Jesus Christ, a prophet and the only human begotten "Son of God" and who claim that he is "God the Son." Apostle Edward

Prayer: *FATHER, help this poor servant of YOURS to only teach YOUR Holy Word and in the process help me refuse to add to it, subtract from it and especially FATHER help me to refuse to read into YOUR Word something that is not there simply because someone or the Church believes it is there. Keep me under YOUR watchful eyes and under YOUR wings. FATHER, have mercy on all Christians who have been deceived by the trinity dogma. Guide them so that they may become lovers of the truth. YOUR truth!*

Lessons Thirty-Nine Through Seventy-Six

39. Jesus teaches he is "Son of Man" but Bible excludes this as an attribute of God.

40. Bible teaches Jesus is a "Man" but Bible excludes this as an attribute of God.

41. Catholic teachings on the trinity dogma are opposite of Catholic Bibles (Word).

42. Trinity doctrine teaches against the teachings of Jesus.

43. Trinity doctrine teaches against the Word of God.

44. The creators of the trinity doctrine at Nicea in 325 AD operated off of hand written manuscripts and did not have the benefit of the complete Canon in printed form for wide distribution.

45. The creators of the trinity doctrine operated off of their human memory and hand written notes and did not have the benefit of Scripture on computer software that makes it easy to search and understand.

46. There are many "sons of God" but only one "begotten Son of God."

47. Whoever is a mother that does the will of the FATHER in Heaven is the mother of Jesus. This is the teaching of Jesus.

48. Mary was the mother of the human being called Jesus. She is not "Mother of God." If this were not true, then Jesus has lied when he taught us who was his mother. Ergo, all mothers who do the will of the FATHER are Jesus' mother(s).

49. Whoever is a woman or man who does the will of the FATHER in Heaven is the sister or brother of Jesus. This is the teaching of Jesus.

50. The fact one is a brother or sister of Jesus makes us a "son of God" or "daughter of God." However, it does not make us "God the Son" or "God the Daughter."

51. The Church created a "God the Son" dogma and it is unscriptural.

52. The Church created a "God the Holy Spirit" dogma and it is unscriptural.

53. The Church created a "Mary, Mother of God" dogma and it is unscriptural.

54. Jesus was an apostle of God.

55. Jesus is now the High Priest of God in Heaven, sitting at God's right hand.

56. Jesus was a prophet of God.

57. Jesus was the "seed of David" in his flesh.

58. Jesus was the "Son of God" in his spirit.

59. Christ was an angel of God before becoming incarnate as Jesus.

60. Christ is an archangel that comes back with the trumpet of God.

61. Jesus is our spiritual rock that is supposed to guide us back to God.

62. Jesus taught us to not ask anything anymore of him.

63. Jesus taught us to take our prayers directly to God, whom he taught was the FATHER.

64. Jesus taught us that after the resurrection he would no longer pray to the FATHER for us, since we could go directly to the FATHER.

65. Jesus taught us to pray to the FATHER in his name if we wanted prayer answered.

66. Jesus said the FATHER loved us because we loved him and that we believed he came from the FATHER who sent him from Heaven.

67. Jesus reaffirms multiple times in Scripture that his and our God is the FATHER.

68. Jesus came from the FATHER.

69. Jesus returned to the FATHER.

70. All who overcome this world believe in the "Son of God" not "God the Son".

71. Don't add anything to God's Word.

72. Don't subtract anything from God's Word.

73. Don't otherwise alter the meaning of God's Word.

74. Fear the prophet who speaks for God and obey God's instructions.

75. The ancient *Book of Enoch* contains a warning for those who pervert God's Word. Their spirits shall be thrust into a pit of fire, which blazes with great suffering.

76. God has given a warning through the Apostle Edward of woes that will befall all who pervert the teachings or our Lord Jesus Christ, changing Jesus as the human begotten "Son of God" and transforming him into an idolatrous "God the Son."

The Man-Made Trinity Dogma Of The Church Is "The" Great End-Times Deception

Christ takes vengeance upon his return

"When the Lord Jesus is revealed from Heaven with HIS mighty angels, in flaming fire taking vengeance on those who [A] do not know God, and on [B] those who do not obey the gospel of our Lord Jesus Christ. These [two groups] shall be punished with everlasting destruction from the presence of the Lord and from the glory of his power, when he comes, in that Day, to be glorified in his saints and to be admired among all those who believe, because our testimony among you was believed."
2 Thessalonians 1: 7-10 (NKJV)

> "When the Lord Jesus shall be revealed from Heaven, with the angels of his power: In a flame of fire, giving vengeance to them who [A] know not God, and [B] who obey not the gospel of our Lord Jesus Christ. Who shall suffer eternal punishment in destruction, from the face of the Lord, and from the glory of his power: When he shall come to be glorified in his saints, and to be made wonderful in all them who have believed; because our testimony was believed upon you in that day." 2 Thessalonians 1: 7-10 (Douay-Rheims)

Christ takes vengeance for God on whom?
- A) On those who do not know God, and
- B) On those who do not obey the gospel of our Lord Jesus

Apostle Paul's Warning

Christ, upon his return, takes vengeance for God on everyone who does not know his God! This is group [A] identified in the above two verses. Now, who did Christ teach us in Scripture was his God? Yes, it's the FATHER. Take heed. It is Apostle Paul that writes this warning in 2 Thessalonians 1:7-10. However, God has burdened this apostle's heart for Christians who have been misled about the nature of God and of his only begotten human Son, Jesus Christ. If you believe in the trinity doctrine, you do not know the God that Jesus served. If you are a righteous trinity believer, this may mitigate your judgment, but this is my best guess and I am unsure about your eternal outcome. You will be picked up at the last day according to the teachings of Jesus that I presented in *"The Messenger."* Jesus will do this because he has promised all who believe in him that he would pick them up on the last day (John 6:39-54). The reason I am unsure of your eternal outcome is the fact that you have failed to learn who God was and in light of the above teaching of Apostle Paul, it clouds the issue. If you are picked up on the last day, you will be judged along with every other soul picked up. Why not learn who God is and believe in what Jesus taught in John 5:24. Consider carefully whether you want to be picked up on the last day as described in *"The Messenger"*, facing an uncertain judgment or if you would like to fall under this second and alternative salvation [eternal life] teaching of Jesus.

> "Most assuredly, I say to you, he who hears my word and believes in HIM who sent me has everlasting life, and shall not come into judgment, but has passed from death into life." John 5:24 (NKJV)

> "Amen, amen I say unto you, that he who heareth my word, and believeth HIM that sent me, hath life everlasting; and cometh not into judgment, but is passed from death to life." John 5:24 (Douay-Rheims)

Knowing Yahweh means having already passed from death into eternal life even while alive on this earth. It means no judgment to those faithful to God. This beats not knowing the God that Jesus served and the uncertain outcome of Jesus' last day pickup plan.

They did not receive the love of God's truth and perished

Apostle Paul continues on with discussion in 2 Thessalonians about a great deception that takes place and the unrighteousness that abounds because people no longer love the truth. And what is the truth? God teaches us that HIS Word is our truth!

>**"Then Jesus said to those Jews who believed him, "If you abide in my word, you are my disciples indeed. And you shall know the truth, and the truth shall make you free." John 8:31-32 (NKJV)**

>**"Then Jesus said to those Jews, who believed him: If you continue in my word, you shall be my disciples indeed. And you shall know the truth, and the truth shall make you free." John 8:31-32 (Douay-Rheims)**

There are five steps to knowing the truth and getting set free

1. Believing in Christ and in the FATHER [his and our God].
2. Abiding and living in Christ's word [the words he received from God].
3. Becoming a disciple of Christ [which is becoming another servant of God].
4. Knowing the truth [not learning but actually "knowing" from God's Spirit].
5. Getting set free by the truth. Giving God's Word priority over Church dogma.

Until you give priority to God's Word over church dogma, in your heart, mind and life, the truth has not set you free. Jesus was talking "to Jews who believed him." Therefore, believing in God and in HIS Son was the very first condition of "knowing" the truth. The Jews would have already believed in Yahweh. A sincere heart is a companion to true and real belief. The above verse in John is another way of saying Christ can open up your mind's understanding to truth. The source of spiritual truth is God's Word. To stand up for HIS truth means that you are rational and you take your emotions out of play. The truth you need to love is God's Word. Only HIS truth will keep you from perishing during the End-Times and falling prey to the spiritual deceptions that are now upon mankind.

>**"Sanctify them by YOUR truth. YOUR word is truth."**
>   **John 17:17 (NKJV)**

>**"Sanctify them in truth. THY word is truth."**
>   **John 17:17 (Douay-Rheims)**

>**"The entirety of YOUR word is truth, and every one of YOUR righteous judgments endures forever." Psalms 119:160 (NKJV)**

>**"YOUR every word is enduring; all YOUR just edicts are forever."**
>   **Psalms 119:160 (NAB)**

God's Truth is found in HIS Holy Word.
Jesus, as prophet of God, only spoke God's Word to us!

Unrighteous deception among those who perish

"The coming of the lawless one is according to the working of Satan, with all power, signs, and lying wonders, and with all <u>unrighteous deception among those who perish</u>, because they did not receive the love of the truth, that they might be saved. And for this <u>reason God will send them strong delusion</u>, that they should believe the lie, that they all may be condemned who did not believe the truth but had pleasure in unrighteousness." 2 Thessalonians 2:9-12 (NKJV)

"Whose coming [lawless one] is according to the working of Satan, in all power, and signs, and lying wonders, and in all <u>seduction of iniquity to them that perish</u>; because they receive not the love of the truth, that they might be saved. <u>Therefore God shall send them the operation of error, to believe lying</u>: That all may be judged who have not believed the truth, but have consented [took pleasure] to [in] iniquity [unrighteousness]." 2 Thessalonians 2:9-11 (Douay-Rheims)

God sends them strong delusion? Error?

I can hear someone saying: "Whoa, wait a minute here. You mean God sends a strong delusion or an operation of error so people will believe a lie?" Well, yes, and it was the Apostle Paul that taught us this. God has asked me to remind Christians of these facts in HIS Word. Ergo, you get another chance to open up your eyes to HIM and HIS Truth.

They received not the love of the Truth!

Paul's warning tells us that the people perished because A) they believed the lie, and; B) they never received the love of the truth. In simple spiritual terms, these people never actually received Jesus Christ in their heart. If they had, they would have been given God's Holy Spirit, which is called the Spirit of Truth. Had their souls been touched by God's Spirit, they would be hungry for God's Word. I know I am. And, talking about HIS Word always gives me a thrill and satisfies my soul in ways I cannot even express.

So, when was the last time you picked up a Bible and read "HIS Truth?" When was the last time you even picked up a Bible to test the veracity of what your pastor or priest has just taught you? The lies abound from the pulpit about God's Word. If you start actually reading the Word and checking what is being said about it, you *may* be astounded at the outright lies and deception coming out of the mouth of your very own pastor or priest. So, how can you receive the love of the truth if you don't <u>abide</u> in it? The answer is you can't. And, what about all the words God is giving you in this book? Will you pick up a Bible and verify them? Will you believe HIS Word? Or, will you set this book aside as being too much in conflict with Church doctrine? Especially the revered trinity doctrine? Being a disciple of Jesus means you are a follower of his teachings. Are you? Have you really received the love of the truth or are you a lover of your Church and its doctrine?

Trinity Dogma © 2009 Rev. Edward G. Palmer

The greatest Church deception is the trinity doctrine

For all the Scriptures I have provided prior to this point and all afterwards, I can say with good confidence that the greatest deception upon Christianity today is the trinity doctrine. Without a doubt there is no support in Scripture and this doctrine actually negates the truth found in Scripture. The trinity doctrine is the fulfillment of prophecy in these last days, when sound doctrine and biblically based instructions will be ignored in favor of teachings that feed the itching ears of Christians. Traditions will be reinforced and in truth, it takes a strong person to stand up and say, "I was wrong." That's what I had to do after five decades of being programmed by the Church. Yet, I am a lover of the truth and have always been one. "Give me the raw truth and just the truth, I can handle it!" As such, I am always on the look out for other lovers of the truth. I want to tell you it is very scary in humanity at large. I have not met many people who are real "lovers of the truth." I know that perhaps millions of people will read this book. God has already made that clear to me. Yet, how many will set this "truth" aside in favor of the social acceptance in their current group of friends within the Church that they now attend?

The Mythology Prophecy

"For the time will come when men will not put up with sound doctrine. Instead, to suit their own desires, they will gather around them a great number of teachers to say what their itching ears want to hear. They will turn their ears away from the truth and aside to myths." 2 Timothy 4:3-4 New International Version (NIV)

The Truth Prophecy

"The coming of the lawless one will be in accordance with the work of Satan displayed in all kinds of counterfeit miracles, signs and wonders, and in every sort of evil that deceives those who are perishing. They perish because they refused to love the truth and so be saved. For this reason God sends them a powerful delusion so that they will believe the lie and so that all will be condemned who have not believed the truth but have delighted in wickedness."
                                      2 Thessalonians 2:9-12 (NIV)

Both Prophecies Fulfilled

"The prophecies in 2 Timothy 4:3-4 and 2 Thessalonians 2:9-12 are fulfilled. Today, mythology is routinely taught from the pulpits of many Christian churches instead of God's Holy Word and many people attending Christian churches have turned away from His truth. These people are headed toward Hell unaware of their lost souls." The Apostle Edward (2005)

Judgment Begins In House of God

Peter said: "For the time has come for judgment to begin at the house of God; and if it begins with us first, what will be the end of those who do not obey the gospel of God?" 1 Peter 4:17 (NKJV)

Peter said: "For the time is, that judgment should begin at the house of God. And if first at us, what shall be the end of them that believe not the gospel of God?" 1 Peter 4:17 (Douay-Rheims)

Warning, Judgment Has Started

"God's judgment has begun in the Church or 'at the house of God' as Peter lamented. Peter's lamentation is a righteous testimony that even in his time, Church leaders misled the people about God. Peter calls for the Church to get its act together before it's too late. Today, the Church routinely teaches mythology with the idolatrous creations of 'God the Son'; 'God the Holy Spirit'; and, 'Mary, Mother of God.' Truly God will repay all who pervert the truth of HIS Word and who lead HIS sheep astray. What will be the end of those who do not obey Jesus and have perverted the teachings he gave us; words he received from God HIMSELF?

WARNING to all Church leaders regardless of denomination. Put your house in order for God before it is too late. Return back to the worship of the God that Jesus and Paul clearly identified for us as the FATHER. Indeed, these are the End-Times and your apostasy will be dealt with by God soon." The Apostle Edward

Worship Only The <u>FATHER</u>;
Stop All Idolatrous Worship <u>Now</u>!

Jesus said: "But the hour is coming, and now is, <u>when true worshippers will worship the FATHER</u> in spirit and truth; for the FATHER is seeking such to worship HIM." John 4:24 (NKJV)

Jesus said: "God is a spirit; and they that adore HIM, must adore HIM in spirit and in truth." John 4:24 (Douay-Rheims)

Jesus said: "God is Spirit, and those who worship HIM must worship in Spirit and truth." John 4:24 (NAB)

Who did Jesus teach us to worship in spirit and truth? God! And, both Jesus and Paul identified God as the FATHER!

Thirty-Three Scriptures From God "To Hear!"

God's Word speaks against the trinity dogma. Yet, God has given me a list of thirty-three Scriptures for you to think about. Not everyone who reads this list will understand, because many cannot hear God. Yet, if you are of God, you will surely hear HIS Word.

"He [or she] who is of God hears God's words; therefore you do not hear, because you are not of God." John 8:47 (NKJV)

Scripture	Synopsis
John 20:17	Jesus identifies the FATHER as his and also as our God.
1 Corinthians 8:3-6	Paul identifies the FATHER as our God.
John 17:3	Jesus says eternal life is to know [Yahweh] and him [Jesus].
Numbers 23:19	God is not a "man" nor is HE a "son of man." These two attributes cannot be attributed to our God, but only to Jesus.
Isaiah 45:21	God [Yahweh] says there is no other God / SAVIOR besides HIM.
Isaiah 44:8	God [Yahweh] says there is no other God besides HIM.
Revelation 21:3	God HIMSELF returns to be with HIS people. Jesus returns earlier.
Psalms 104:4	God made the angel's spirits. That includes Christ's spirit.
Psalms 106:21	They forgot God, their Savior. (Speaks of Egypt and also today).
Proverbs 30:5-6	Do not add to God's Word. That includes reading in extra stuff.
Isaiah 7:15	As a child, Jesus was fed curds and honey so he would know to refuse the evil and choose the good. Jesus *grew* in knowledge.
Isaiah 40:5	God shows HIS glory to all flesh [on HIS return]. God returns.
Isaiah 42:8	I am the LORD, that is MY name; And MY glory I will not give to another, Nor MY praise to carved images.
John 5:19	Jesus cannot do anything of his own accord.
John 5:24-30	Those who believe in the FATHER have eternal life, no judgment. Jesus has been given authority to grant salvation by the FATHER. Jesus does nothing on his own, but executes the FATHER'S will.
John 5:39-44	I come in my FATHER'S name and you do not receive me. Today, Jesus would say: I come in my FATHER'S name and you do not receive HIM as our only God!
John 6:38	I come down from Heaven to do the will of HIM who sent me.

Trinity Dogma © 2009 Rev. Edward G. Palmer

John 6:57	Jesus said, "I live because of the FATHER."
John 8:42	I proceeded forth and came from God. If he were also your FATHER, you would love me.
John 14:1	You believe in God, believe also in me. Today it would be reversed. Jesus would say: You believe in me, believe also in my FATHER who is our God.
John 14:28	My FATHER is greater than I am. I go to the FATHER. If you love Jesus, you would rejoice that he is going to the FATHER.
John 16:28	Jesus came forth from God and returns back to God.
John 17:6	Jesus manifested God's name to disciples who kept God's word.
Ephesians 1:17	The "God of our Lord Jesus Christ, the FATHER of glory."
Philippians 2:6-9	God exalted Jesus and gave him a name above all others.
Colossians 1:15	Christ was the firstborn of all creation.
1 Timothy 2:5	One God and one mediator, the "man" Christ Jesus.
Hebrews 2:17	Jesus had to be "made" like all other human males.
Hebrews 10:9	Jesus came to do "God's" will.
1 Peter 1:21-22	Who through Jesus, we believe in God. Our faith and hope is in God as a result of truly accepting Jesus Christ in our hearts.
1 John 4:3	The spirit of the antichrist denies that Christ came "in the flesh."
Revelation 3:1	There are seven spirits of God and the Holy Spirit is only one of the seven. Jesus was given all seven of God's Spirits.
Revelation 3:14	Jesus is the "beginning" of God's creation / God's "first creation."

Now Listen To Apostle Peter

"[Jesus] indeed was foreordained before the foundation of the world, but was manifest in these last times for you who through [Jesus] believe in God, who raised [Jesus] from the dead and gave [Jesus] glory, so that your faith and hope are in God." 1 Peter 1:21-22 (NKJV)

"Who through him are faithful in God, who raised him up from the dead, and hath given him glory, that your faith and hope might be in God." 1 Peter 1:21-22 (Douay-Rheims)

"You who through Jesus believe in God,
So that your faith and hope are in God HIMSELF!"

Think about it!

Lessons Seventy-Seven through One-Hundred-Seven

77. Upon his return, Christ takes vengeance on all who do not know his God.
78. Upon his return, Christ takes vengeance on all who do not obey his gospel.
79. Apostle Paul warned us of Christ's vengeance in 2 Thessalonians.
80. Christ promised to pick up all who believe in him on the last day.
81. Everyone picked up on the last day will go through a judgment.
82. Christ also taught that those who believed in Yahweh [HIM who sent me] have already passed into eternal life and bypassed judgment.
83. Christ teaches two eternal life or salvation scenarios for those who believe in him.
84. It is doubtful that those who believe in the trinity really know Jesus. In John 12:44, Jesus explains that true belief in him means people believe in his God.
85. People perish during the End-Times because they are not lovers of the truth.
86. The Bible teaches that God's Word is the truth.
87. Few people read God's Word. Ergo, few people know God's truth.
88. Jesus describes five distinct steps to actually "knowing" the truth.
89. Those who have truly accepted Jesus will have the Spirit of Truth inside of them.
90. Very few people on earth are actually "lovers of the truth."
91. Those who are lovers of the truth give God's Word priority over Church dogma.
92. Jesus in fulfilling his role as a prophet only spoke God's Word to us.
93. Spiritual deceptions abound during these last days.
94. Unrighteous deceptions abound during these last days.
95. God sends a strong delusion so those who would not believe the truth perish.
96. The trinity doctrine is a strong delusion because the Bible speaks against it.
97. Many people love the Church over and above God's Word.
98. Paul prophesied that in the End-Times, men would turn to mythology.
99. Paul prophesied that in the End-Times, men would turn away from truth.
100. In 2005, Apostle Edward declared that Paul's prophecies have come true.
101. Judgment begins in the house of God, the Church.
102. A warning has been issued to the Church to set its house in order.
103. True worshippers worship only the FATHER in spirit and truth.
104. Worship of "God the Son"; "God the Holy Spirit"; and, "Mary, Mother of God" is idolatrous in God's eyes, given HIS Holy Scriptures.

Trinity Dogma © 2009 Rev. Edward G. Palmer

105. God has provided thirty-three distinct Scripture references in the table above that speak directly against the trinity doctrine. The rows above the solid line contain seven Scriptures that speak *strongly* against the trinity dogma.

106. Apostle Peter taught us that we would believe in God through the efforts of Jesus.

107. Apostle Peter taught that as a result of Jesus, our "faith and hope would be placed in God HIMSELF." Ergo, true belief in Jesus leads us to turn to our God!

Belief in Jesus <u>should</u> lead people to turn to God!

Didn't belief in Moses lead people to turn to God? Or do you think Moses led people to believe that Jesus was their God?

Think about it!

Church Money Grabbing Tradition

Now, let's return to Matthew 15 for a moment and examine more closely what the Church was changing by their tradition that Jesus talked about. Remember? The Church negated God's commandments with their tradition?

In the illustration at Matthew 15:3, Jesus is referring to how church authorities gave the "okay" for people to give all their money to the church. In this case, authorities taught that giving to the church was the same as giving to God. Ergo, giving to the Church was "equivalent" to giving to God HIMSELF. Sound familiar? When found broke and unable to help their father or mother as a result, they were told to tell their parents that they gave all their money "as a gift to God." Of course, this meant they were unable to "honor" their parents as God commanded. This money instruction negated God's commandment.

The Church money teaching made God's Word of no effect to the members of the congregation who were ignorant of the Word. For God, it was like HE had never given us the instruction to "honor our father and mother." Yes, it was *still* in HIS written word, but Church leaders had subverted HIS Word. Of course, this was all about confiscating the money people had to help their family. Whatever little amount it was, the Church wanted it. So, in Jesus' time then, people were made to feel good about "giving all their money [or assets] to the church," even if it meant they would not honor their parents.

It's about 2,000 years since Jesus admonished the authorities about negating God's commandments with their "teaching as doctrines the commandments of men!" You might have thought that this particular "man-made" *money* doctrine and lie had ceased by now. However, it is still alive and well having morphed into the modern Church tithe doctrine.

The sad truth is many Charismatic, Pentecostal and other denominations [even at least one mainline Lutheran church that I know] routinely preach a similar message when it comes to raising money for the church coffers. A full discussion of the money grab called "tithing" is online in the *Book of Edward*. Go to http://www.edwardtheapostle.org and select Volume III, Itching Christian Ears. After that, select Chapter 17 titled [it's a] *"Myth—Giving 10% is a Tithe."*

The modern Church money doctrine called tithing also negates God's commandment to honor our father and mother and take care of your family. I don't, however, believe the Catholic Church is a participant and certainly not a promoter. I have attended Mass for a few months now and I have never heard a tithe pitch or for that matter any other money grabbing sales pitch. In part, there is simply not enough time to promote such a doctrine during Mass, which is a highly structured worship service. It is to the Catholic Church credit that they do not abuse God's Word in this manner like the many protestant churches I am aware of. You cannot serve both God and money.

The modern tithe apostasy covertly teaches Christians to serve money instead of God, because the focus of this teaching and all that surrounds it is based on obtaining worldly things and not the things of God. Ergo, the basic message is that you can name it and then claim it. Whatever you want, God will give it to you. You just need to know how to ask and make sure you are first tithing. And, of course, God won't honor your prayers if you don't tithe. In fact, HE may curse you if you don't tithe. Or, how about this pitch: God wants HIS kids to have all the diamonds, luxury cars, yachts or any other worldly thing they can name and claim? The tithe message is satanic and an abuse of God's Holy Word.

For the record, the AFCM or *Association of Faith Church Ministries* is the worse offender and promoter of this false man-made money doctrine. They are also known as *Word of Faith* churches. You will also find Pentecostal churches like the *Assemblies of God* promoting the doctrine. Such teachings reflect either profound ignorance of God's Word or the teachings of one of Satan's servants and not God's servant. Harsh? It's the kindest words I can say. Tithe preachers are either woefully ignorant of Scripture or they are a servant of Satan. It's simply one of those two conditions. Now, lets talk about God's second commandment concerning our worship and whether or not the Catholic Church is engaged in idolatrous teachings and behavior with the use of "carved images."

Church Carved Image Tradition

When it comes to the Roman Catholic Church, there is the **not-so-small** issue of actually deleting and ignoring the second commandment of God from their list of commandments. Yes, Jesus taught that man [or the Church] would negate or change the meaning of God's commandments through the teachings of their own traditions "as commandments." This is illustrated in the money tradition of Matthew 15 and the discussion above. But, could this apostasy extend to deleting and ignoring one of God's ten commandments? The answer is yes. That is exactly what the Roman Catholic Church has done with the second commandment of God. Let me explain why Catholics may be in spiritual hot water.

Note: Unless otherwise noted, all references to the Catholic Church in this book refer to the Roman Catholic Church. An Internet search will reveal that there are several other Catholic churches, which are not affiliated with or part of the Roman Catholic Church. The Pope is the head of the Roman Catholic Church. This is the Catholic Church I am talking about in the discussions of this book.

While the Catholic Church is the center of the discussion now, it should be noted that Lutheran and other denominations that broke away from the Catholic Church still carry with them some of their traditions. It is noteworthy that Martin Luther never did realize that the Catholic Church had deleted the second commandment and split the tenth commandment in two to make a total of ten. This is an interesting fact in and of itself.

God's Second Commandment

You will find the commandments that God gave Moses in Exodus 20:1-17 and Deuteronomy 5:6-21. The second commandment appears as follows in the Bible.

> "**You shall not make** for yourself **any carved image**, or for yourself **anything that is in Heaven above**, or that is in the earth beneath, or that is in the water under the earth; you **shall not bow down to them** nor serve them. For I, the LORD your God, am a jealous God, visiting the iniquity of the fathers on the children to the third and fourth generations of those who hate ME, but showing mercy to thousands, to those who love ME and keep MY commandments."
>
> **Exodus 20:4-5 (NKJV)**

> "**You shall not make** for yourself **any carved image**, or any likeness **of anything that is in Heaven above**, or that is in the earth beneath, or that is in the water under the earth; you shall not bow down to them nor serve them. For I, the LORD your God, am a jealous God, visiting the iniquity of the fathers upon the children to the third and fourth generations of those who hate ME, but showing mercy to thousands, to those who love ME and keep MY commandments."
>
> **Deuteronomy 5:8-10 (NKJV)**

God's second commandment commands that we:

1. **Don't make any carved image**
    a. Of the likeness of anything in Heaven
    b. Of the likeness of anything on the earth
    c. Of the likeness of anything under the earth

2. **Do not bow down to any carved image**
    a. Of the likeness of anything in Heaven
    b. Of the likeness of anything on the earth
    c. Of the likeness of anything under the earth

God also makes it clear that HE will have mercy on those who love HIM and keep HIS commandments. That includes not creating any carved images nor bowing down to any carved image. This literally means *any* image! The *New King James Version* uses the word "carved" and the *Douay-Rheims Bible* and the *King James Bible* both use the word "graven." The word *graven* means, "to engrave or sculpt on the surface an image" and is easily translated "carved." The word "image," however, does translate directly to "idol" and represents a changed subject [carved image/graven thing v. idol]. Most newer bible translations read, "carve idols" as does the *New American Bible* verses shown below.

> "**Thou shalt not make** to thyself **a graven thing, nor the likeness of any thing that is in Heaven above**, or in the earth beneath, nor of those things that are in the waters under the earth. Thou shalt not adore them, nor serve them: I am the LORD thy God, mighty, jealous, visiting the iniquity of the fathers upon the children, unto the third and fourth generation of them that hate ME: And shewing mercy unto thousands to them that love ME, and keep my commandments."
> Exodus 20:4-6 (Douay-Rheims)

> "Thou shalt not make to thyself **a graven thing**, nor the likeness of any things, that are in Heaven above, or that are in the earth beneath, or that abide in the waters under the earth. Thou shalt not adore them, and thou shalt not serve them. For I am the LORD thy God, a jealous God, visiting the iniquity of the fathers upon their children unto the third and fourth generation, to them that hate ME, and shewing mercy unto many thousands, to them that love ME, and keep my commandments." Deuteronomy 5:8-10 (Douay-Rheims)

Carved Images Vs. Carved Idols

> "**You shall not carve idols** for yourselves in the shape of anything in the sky above or on the earth below or in the waters beneath the earth; you shall not bow down before them or worship them."
> Exodus 20:4-5 (NAB)

> "**You shall not carve idols** for yourselves in the shape of anything in the sky above or on the earth below or in the waters beneath the earth; you **shall not bow down before them** or worship them."
> Deuteronomy 5:8-9 (NAB)

On the surface, it would seem we have two distinct meanings in these translations. In one instance, God commands us "to not carve any images [graven thing] period." In a second, we have an instruction not to "carve idols." If the truth is the former, then virtually every Catholic Church is guilty of violating God's second commandment through the use of an image of "Jesus crucified on the cross" in the form of a Crucifix hanging behind a hewed altar with a statue of Mary to Jesus' right and a statue of Joseph to Jesus' left.

The issue gets more complicated as Catholics are taught to bow down before the Crucifix upon entering and exiting their pews. Catholics also kneel before the Crucifix several times during the service. And, whenever any function is performed before the altar, Catholics bow before the crucifix/altar before and after the function has been performed.

Would God consider this bowing down to a carved image in violation of His command? Certainly the Catholic Church would not consider its hanging Crucifix to be an idol. Every Catholic knows you don't bow down to idols. Yet, would God view this worship practice the same as Catholics? Well, I'm curious, so let's consider a few translations and how the second commandment reads. Is it "carved images [graven thing]" or "carved idols?" Deuteronomy 5:8-10 is used for comparative purposes. Exodus reflects the same.

#	Translation	Image or Graven Thing	Idols
1	New King James Version	✔	
2	Douay-Rheims	✔	
3	King James Version	✔	
4	New American Bible		✔
5	American Standard Version	✔	
6	Amplified Bible	✔	
7	Bible In Basic English	✔	
8	Contemporary English Version		✔
9	Darby's Translation	✔	
10	English Standard Version	✔	
11	Geneva Bible	✔	
12	God's Word		✔
13	Holman Christian Standard Bible		✔
14	International Children's Bible		✔
15	Jewish Study Bible Tanakh	✔	
16	New American Standard Bible		✔
17	New American Standard Bible 1977		✔
18	New Century Version		✔
19	New English Translation (NET)	✔	
20	New International Version		✔
21	New Jerusalem Bible	✔	
22	New Living Translation		✔
23	New Revised Standard Version		✔
24	Revised English Bible	✔	
25	Revised Standard Version	✔	
26	The Living Bible		✔
27	The Message		✔
28	The Stone Edition Tanach	✔	
29	Today's English Version	✔	
30	Young's Literal Translation	✔	
31	James Moffatt Translation		✔
		17 (54.8%)	14 (45.2%)

Analysis: In general the older translations cited "carved image or graven thing" and the newer ones cited "idols," but this is not always the case. The *James Moffatt Translation*, an older one, cited "idols." And, the *NET Bible*, a newer translation with translator's notes cited "images." A combining of the two might get, "Don't make any carved images of an idol." Yet, isn't this much [the image part] implicit in the statement, "You shall not carve idols?" Idols do contain an image and the word change only changes the subject [noun].

There is a nuance here that should not go unnoticed as it relates to the Crucifix and the statues adjacent to it that Catholics bow down to. From a theology perspective, if the verse translates "idols," then it must be okay to have the Crucifix and statues at the altar for people to bow down to, because everyone knows we don't worship these carved images, don't they? Everyone knows that they are really not "carved idols?" I am not so sure if all the Catholic leadership viewed it this way initially when they started using the Crucifix and other images, authorized in 787 AD by the seventh ecumenical council at Nicea. There is no doubt a rationale for using all the images, but what about God?

What does God think about the image and icon use? It is the second commandment of God, missing in Catholic literature and the splitting of the tenth commandment into two parts to get "Ten" that inherently <u>smells</u> before God of Church duplicity and sin. The Church cannot claim it doesn't violate God's second commandment while deleting it and then making up for the deletion by splitting the ninth commandment into two parts. It is self-evident and prima facie evidence of duplicity and sin in God's point of view.

The Missing Second Commandment

In the *Saint Joseph New American Catechism No. 3 Illustrated*, Catholic Book Publishing Co., NY (1970), p 232, we see the following list of the "Ten Commandments of God."

1. I, the LORD, am your God. You shall have no other gods besides me.
2. You shall not take the name of the LORD, your God, in vain.
3. Remember to keep holy the Sabbath day.
4. Honor your father and your mother.
5. You shall not kill.
6. You shall not commit adultery.
7. You shall not steal.
8. You shall not bear false witness against your neighbor.
9. You shall not covet your neighbor's wife.
10. You shall not covet anything that belongs to your neighbor.

The same list appears in *Basic Catechism*, St. Paul Books & Media, Boston, MA (1970), p150, published by the Daughters of St. Paul. And, this list appears in many other books referencing Catholic theology.

The same list of Ten Commandments appears in a Lutheran confirmation book. *The Junior Confirmation Book*, Augsburg Publishing House, Minneapolis, MN (1943). See the list of Ten Commandments starting on p181. Ergo, Martin Luther missed the split.

An Outside View Of Catholic Mass

The Apostle Paul, when writing about tongues in 1 Corinthians, writes about what an uninformed or unbeliever [or outsider] might think of everyone speaking in tongues.

> **"Therefore tongues are for a sign, not to those who believe but to unbelievers; but prophesying is not for unbelievers but for those who believe. Therefore if the whole church comes together in one place, and all speak with tongues [at the same time], and there come in those who are uninformed or unbelievers [or an outsider], will they not say that you are out of your mind?" I Corinthians 14:22-23 (NKJV)**

My own family experienced such an occasion, visiting a small Four-Square church in California many years ago, when everyone in the church all started speaking in tongues. Yes, our reaction was exactly as Paul predicted. We thought they were all nuts and out of their minds. And, at the time, I believed in speaking in tongues. Today, I do speak in tongues. Yet, the issue isn't whether or not you believe in this gift of the spirit. The issue is what an outsider would think. So, what would an outsider think of Catholic Mass? An outsider who both knew and truly believed in God's second commandment? Step outside the box of the Catholic worship service. Put yourself in the shoes of an objective outsider. What do you see happening? What do you observe during Mass? Would you:

1. See one or more "carved or graven images" at the altar?
2. See a Crucifix of Christ on the cross at the altar as the center worship image?
3. See a statue or image of Mary to the right of Jesus on the cross?
4. See a statue of image of Joseph to the left of Jesus on the cross?
5. See Catholics bowing down to this center altar image of the Crucifix?
6. See Catholics bowing down during various functions of the worship service?
7. Believe that Catholics are committing idolatry in the eyes of God?

If Catholics do not bow down to the Crucifix and other images, whom do they bow down to? God? It can't be HIM, because God's Word teaches us HE does not occupy man-made structures. God dwells in "the high and holy place" and HE also inhabits the praises of HIS people. And, Jesus taught us God's kingdom was to be found inside of us [our heart].

> **"For thus saith the HIGH and the EMINENT that inhabiteth eternity: and HIS name is HOLY, <u>WHO dwelleth</u> in the high and holy place, and with a contrite and humble spirit, to revive the spirit of the humble, and to revive the heart of the contrite." Isaiah 57:15 (Douay-Rheims)**

> **"God, who made the world, and all things therein; HE, being LORD of Heaven and earth, <u>dwelleth not</u> in temples [buildings] made with [human] hands." Acts 17:24 (Douay-Rheims)**

> **"But THOU art holy, O THOU that <u>inhabitest</u> [dwells within] the praises of [your people] Israel." Psalms 22:3 (KJV)**

Trinity Dogma © 2009 Rev. Edward G. Palmer

> "And being asked by the Pharisees, when the kingdom of God should come? He [Jesus] answered them, and said: The kingdom of God cometh not with observation: Neither shall they say: Behold here, or behold there [as in a church building]. For lo, <u>the kingdom of God is within you</u>." Luke 17:21-22 (Douay-Rheims)
>
> Jesus said: "The FATHER <u>who dwells in me</u> is doing HIS works."
> John 14:10 (NAB)
>
> "Do you not know that <u>you are the temple of God</u>, and that the Spirit of <u>God dwells in you</u>?" 1 Corinthians 3:16 (NAB)

The Catholic rationalization for the use of icons and images that they bow down to is that the object of their worship is not the image, but whom the image represents. However, in this case, Jesus *is* the god of the Catholic Church [and all Orthodox churches]. Yet, given the teachings of Jesus that he is not "our" God, the Crucifix in and of itself represents more than just a mere image, statue or cross with Jesus on it. The Crucifix at the altar and whom people bow down to is indeed an idol in the eyes of God. It is idolatry and a willful violation of HIS second commandment. *Woe to those who led God's people astray.*

Even man-hewed altars are objectionable to God. Why? They are not HIS creation. Our God is a jealous God and we ought to consider carefully what HE has instructed us to do.

The Catholic rationalization for the renumbering of the commandments is essentially that others have done the same. Even today, the Lutherans maintain the exact same number of the commandments as previously shown. However, when all is said, the Catholic Church has indeed cloaked the second commandment of God, as it forbids the use of images in any worship service. With this second commandment cloaked, the Church authorized the use of images and icons in the worship service [Mass] in 787 AD. God is *still* not impressed. And, because other people bow down to "images," should you?

Be Still To Know God

> "Be still and see that I am God; I will be exalted among the nations, and I will be exalted in the earth." Psalms 45:11 (Douay-Rheims)

If you want God inside of you, then accept Christ as your savior and obey his teachings. Without obedience, you will never have God indwelling with you. You may already know what this feels like when you are in the presence of true believers; true servants of God. It's that certain "good" feeling you get when you enter a church. You can feel God's Spirit. Indeed, I feel HIM all over my body at this very moment. Yet in other churches there is nothing at all you can "feel" or sense. This has come to be understood as being a "dead" church meaning you can't feel anything. Get a bunch of true believers together for worship and the service can start to get exciting, especially if the Holy Spirit is allowed some freedom. That is where God is found. HE'S inside of those believers; HE'S not in any building per se. That is why a doctrine that teaches bowing down to an image, an actual idol in terms of Jesus' own teaching about who his God was, is idolatrous in God's eyes.

Jesus and Paul teach that the "FATHER is God!"

"But not everyone knows this!" 1 Corinthians 8:7

#	Thirty-One Translations	Jesus teaches: FATHER is God John 20:17	Paul teaches: FATHER is God 1 Cor 8:6
1	New King James Version	✔	✔
2	Douay-Rheims	✔	✔
3	King James Version	✔	✔
4	New American Bible	✔	✔
5	American Standard Version	✔	✔
6	Amplified Bible	✔	✔
7	Bible In Basic English	✔	✔
8	Contemporary English Version	✔	✔
9	Darby's Translation	✔	✔
10	English Standard Version	✔	✔
11	Geneva Bible	✔	✔
12	God's Word	✔	✔
13	Holman Christian Standard Bible	✔	✔
14	International Children's Bible	✔	✔
15	Phillips NT Bible*	✔	✔
16	New American Standard Bible	✔	✔
17	New American Standard Bible 1977	✔	✔
18	New Century Version	✔	✔
19	New English Translation (NET)	✔	✔
20	New International Version	✔	✔
21	New Jerusalem Bible	✔	✔
22	New Living Translation	✔	✔
23	New Revised Standard Version	✔	✔
24	Revised English Bible	✔	✔
25	Revised Standard Version	✔	✔
26	The Living Bible	✔	✔
27	The Message	✔	✔
28	Wesley New Testament*	✔	✔
29	Today's English Version	✔	✔
30	Young's Literal Translation	✔	✔
31	James Moffatt Translation	✔	✔
	*Substitute for Jewish Tanach in first table.	**100% Agreement**	**100% Agreement**

"There is <u>only one God</u>, <u>the FATHER</u>. Everything came from HIM, and we live for HIM. There is only one Lord, Jesus Christ. Everything came into being through him, and we live because of him. <u>But not everyone knows this.</u>" 1 Corinthians 8:6-7 (God's Word)

Trinity Dogma © 2009 Rev. Edward G. Palmer

A "God the FATHER" Scripture Search

You might say, well, of course I believe that God is the FATHER. Even the Catholic Church believes that. Yet, I am not just saying believe in "God the FATHER." What I am saying is that you understand that <u>God is only the FATHER</u>! And, why do I say that? It is because that is what both Jesus and Paul taught us. They are not the ones teaching a man-made doctrine that is opposed to the simple language of Scripture. It is the Church that teaches against Scripture. If "God the Son" and "God the Holy Spirit" and even "Mary, Mother of God" were biblically sound teachings, wouldn't you be able to find these phrases within a Scripture search? Yes, God would not leave such a gap in the Word!

Search Scriptures all you want, but you will not find these dogmatic phrases about the nature of God. The phrase "God the Son", God the Holy Spirit" and "Mary, Mother of God" do not exist within the context of God's Holy Word. However, you *will* find **"God the FATHER"** in a Scripture search. And, why not, this is what Jesus taught his disciples! Consider the following **seventeen teachings found in the <u>Catholic *Douay-Rheims* Bible</u>.** Read them carefully and see if you think they speak of anyone but the FATHER as being our *one* God. Note especially the relationship to Jesus in these verses.

1. John 6:27 "Labour not for the meat which perisheth, but for that which endureth unto everlasting life, which the Son of man will give you. For him hath **God, the FATHER** sealed.

2. 1 Corinthians 8:6 "Yet to us there is but one **God, the FATHER**, of whom are all things, and we unto him; and one Lord Jesus Christ, by whom are all things."

3. Galatians 1:1 "Paul, an apostle, not of men, neither by man, but by Jesus Christ, and **God the FATHER**, who raised him [Jesus] from the dead."

4. Galatians 1:3 "Grace be to you, and peace from **God the FATHER**, and from our Lord Jesus Christ."

5. Ephesians 1:2 "Grace be to you, and peace from **God the FATHER**, and from the Lord Jesus Christ."

6. Ephesians 6:23 "Peace be to the brethren and charity with faith, from **God the FATHER**, and the Lord Jesus Christ.

7. Philippians 2:11 "And that every tongue should confess that the Lord Jesus Christ is in the glory of **God the FATHER.**

8. Colossians 1:12 "Giving thanks to **God the FATHER**, who hath made us worthy to be partakers of the lot of the saints in light."

9. Colossians 2:2 "That their hearts may be comforted, being instructed in charity [love], and unto all riches of fullness of understanding, unto the knowledge of the mystery of **God the FATHER** and of Christ Jesus.

10. 1 Thessalonians 1:1 "Paul and Sylvanus and Timothy: to the church of the Thessalonians, in **God the FATHER**, and in the Lord Jesus Christ."

11. 1 Timothy 1:2 "To Timothy, his beloved son in faith. Grace, mercy, and peace from **God the FATHER**, and from Christ Jesus our Lord."

12. 2 Timothy 1:2 "To Timothy my dearly beloved son, grace, mercy and peace, from **God the FATHER**, and from Christ Jesus our Lord.

13. Titus 1:4 "To Titus my beloved son, according to the common faith, grace and peace from **God the FATHER**, and from Christ Jesus our Lord."

14. 1 Peter 1:2 "According to the foreknowledge of **God the FATHER**, unto the sanctification of the Spirit, unto obedience and sprinkling of the blood of Jesus Christ: Grace unto you and peace be multiplied."

15. 2 Peter 1:17 "For he received from **God the FATHER**, honour and glory: this voice coming down to him from the excellent glory: This is my beloved Son, in whom I am well pleased; hear ye him."

16. 2 John 1:3 "Grace be with you, mercy, and peace from **God the FATHER**, and from Christ Jesus the Son of the FATHER; in truth and charity [love]."

17. Jude 1:1 "Jude, the servant of Jesus Christ, and brother of James: to them that are beloved in **God the FATHER**, and preserved in Jesus Christ, and called."

<u>Who knew</u> that God was *only* the FATHER?

1. Jesus
2. Apostle Paul
3. Apostle John
4. Apostle Peter
5. Apostle Jude
6. Timothy
7. Titus
8. James
9. Sylvanus
10. Thessalonians
11. Colossians
12. Ephesians
13. Philippians
14. Galatians
15. Corinthians
16. <u>Others knew, but not everyone knew.</u> (1 Corinthians 8:7)
17. <u>**Not**</u> the Roman Catholic Church, Lutheran Church and other churches in 2009.

The Gospel Jesus Taught To Paul

Jesus said to Paul: "I will deliver you from the Jewish people, as well as from the Gentiles, to whom I now send you, to <u>open their eyes</u>, in order to <u>turn them from darkness to light</u>, and <u>from the power of Satan to God,</u> <u>that they may receive</u> forgiveness of sins and an inheritance among those who are sanctified by faith in me." Acts 26:17 (NKJV)

Jesus said to Paul: "I shall deliver you from this people and from the Gentiles to whom I send you, to open their eyes that they may turn from darkness to light and from the power of Satan to God, so that they may obtain forgiveness of sins and an inheritance among those who have been consecrated by faith in me." Acts 26:17 (NAB)

<u>Jesus' Gospel</u>

A) Open the people's eyes
B) Turn them from darkness to light
C) Turn them from the power of Satan to [that of] God
D) Then, [if A-C is accomplished] they may receive forgiveness of sins and an inheritance among those who are sanctified by faith in [Jesus].

Jesus taught people to turn to God, his God. The God that Jesus stated clearly was the FATHER. Jesus also taught Paul to teach the very same thing. People are <u>turned</u> to God through their belief and faith in Jesus, HIS only human begotten Son.

> **Apostle James said: "Therefore I judge that we should not trouble those from among the Gentiles *who are turning to God*."**
> **Acts 15:19 (NKJV)**

> **Apostle James said: "For which cause I judge that they, who from among the Gentiles *are converted to God*, are not to be disquieted."**
> **Acts 15:19 (Douay-Rheims)**

<u>Jesus' Gospel</u>

a) **Turned people to God**
b) **Converted people to God**

James' teaching is the same as Peter's. We are "<u>turned to God</u>" as a result of having Jesus in our hearts. Ergo, we don't turn to Jesus! We turn to [or return to] God because of our faith in Jesus! The Church, in perverting God's Word, has many people now turning to "the god Jesus" instead of the God Jesus taught us to turn to. Ergo, many Christians are engaged in idolatrous worship of a "god of love" they call Jesus. This violates the first commandment of a jealous God who taught us not to have any other gods besides HIM. That would include not substituting HIS only human begotten Son Jesus as our God!

Trinity Dogma © 2009 Rev. Edward G. Palmer

Don't Interpret Scripture Using Trinity Doctrine!

When the Hubble space telescope was launched, they soon found out that the mirror lens was not fully polished and finished properly. As a result, the lens distorted everything the Hubble telescope looked at. It was a "built-in" distortion of everything viewed. It is the same way with the Church doctrine of the trinity. It distorts virtually everything you read about God's nature in Holy Scripture. This is Satan's purpose with the doctrine. Examples abound in all of the trinity rationalizations that have ever been written. For example:

1. Many read in Scripture where Jesus says, "I and the FATHER are one" and because of the trinity doctrine they then believe that Jesus and God are both equal and both God. Yet, they ignore John 20:17 where Jesus identifies clearly who God is and many other Scriptures that make it clear Jesus never claimed to be God or even equal with God. They ignore the spiritual words that Jesus used. Even the one where man and his wife are one flesh. This also speaks of a spiritual oneness. It's the same as the Scripture facts that I am Christ's brother and also a "son of God." Yet, this doesn't make me God! In all of these teachings, Christ speaks about the oneness of Spirit that those who are truly of God have with God. It is the same oneness that Christ has with God. Ergo, I can say, "I and the FATHER are one!" Blasphemous? No! This is the spiritual teaching of Jesus in the New Testament!

   Jesus said: "I in them, and YOU in me; that they may be made perfect in one, and that the world may know that YOU have sent me, and have loved them as YOU have loved me." John 17:23 (NKJV)

   "Jesus answered and said to him, "If anyone loves me, he will keep my word; and my FATHER will love him, and we will come to him and make our home with him." John 14:23 (NKJV)

   Jesus said, "It is the Spirit who gives life; the flesh profits nothing. <u>The words that I speak to you are spirit</u>, and they are life." John 6:63 (NKJV)

   Therefore, even I can say, "I and my FATHER are one!" Apostle Edward

2. Many read in Scripture where Jesus says, "I am the way, the truth, and the life. No one comes to the FATHER except through me" and falsely conclude that there is no salvation outside of Jesus Christ. Yet these too were spiritual words and have to be interpreted in light of Ezekiel chapter 18. In Ezekiel, God makes it clear that all who turn away from sin will be saved. Likewise all righteous people who turn to wickedness will be rejected. We also need to take into account Jesus' teaching that no one can come to him unless the FATHER draws him. A correct Bible salvation doctrine must recognize Jesus' teaching about repentance. A careful study of what Jesus taught in light of God's conversation with Ezekiel will reveal that ***the true key to salvation lies in a repentant heart and a return to God.*** This is what Jesus taught. Everyone *will* go through Jesus, because the line forms to his right side!

To conclude that there is no salvation outside of Christ makes God HIMSELF a liar in Ezekiel 18. To conclude that all you have to do is call on Jesus' name for salvation makes Jesus a liar in Matthew 7:21-23. Once again, a doctrine cannot be established without taking into account all of God's Word. And, if a doctrine based upon a Scripture verse is contradicted by another Scripture verse, it is not from God but is a man-made doctrine. Now, regarding the phrase "I am the way," consider carefully what Peter has taught about getting "born-again" of the Spirit *through the word of God.* Ergo, the "way" that Jesus presented to mankind was a reaffirmation of God's Word. Jesus spoke God's Word to us through HIS Spirit.

Peter said: "Since you have purified your souls in obeying the truth through the Spirit in sincere love of the brethren, love one another fervently with a pure heart, having been <u>born again</u>, not of corruptible seed but incorruptible, <u>through the word of God</u> which lives and abides forever, because all flesh is as grass, and all the glory of man as the flower of the grass. The grass withers, and its flower falls away, but the word of the LORD endures forever. Now this is the word which by the gospel was preached to you." 1 Peter 22-25 (NKJV)

We are only born-again through the word of God. <u>All</u> of it!

The "way" that Jesus claimed to be was actually God's Word. That is what Jesus represented to us, as he only spoke and did what God told him to do. If you follow Jesus, you would automatically follow the "way" of God's Word and you would then become "born-again through the word of God" as Peter taught. The word of God leads you home. Ergo, we are not "born-again" by mouthing Jesus as Lord!

3 The New Testament does not eliminate the Old Testament. Virtually all mentions of "Scripture" in the New Testament refer to the words of the Old Testament. Ergo, when the Bereans searched Scripture to see if Paul was telling the truth, they searched the Old Testament. The reason such a doctrine exists is to reinforce the trinity doctrine by eliminating the God found in the Old Testament. Anyone who knows Scripture, will know that Jesus taught, "not one tittle of the law has been done away with" and that Jesus "was the fulfillment of God's law."

Jesus said: "Do not think that I am come to destroy the law, or the prophets. I am not come to destroy, but to fulfill. For amen I say unto you, till Heaven and earth pass, one jot, or one tittle shall not pass of the law, till all be fulfilled." Matthew 5:17-18 (Douay-Rheims)

4 Many read John 8:58 where Jesus says: "Before Abraham was made, I am" and because of the trinity doctrine *read into the Bible* that this verse absolutely means Jesus was God. After all, didn't God use the phrase "I AM" when he told Moses HIS name? Yes HE did but this teaching of Jesus speaks of Elohim or the family of God and not of God HIMSELF. Every word that Jesus uttered is true in light of the fact he existed before Abraham did. However, this verse cannot be interpreted based on God's statement to Moses while ignoring the context of Jesus' words.

Anyone who claims John 8:58 means Jesus is God *makes* Jesus a liar in John 20:17 where he identified his and our God. What John 8:58 does not say is just as significant as what it does say. The trinity doctrine seeks to take Jesus' statement of *I am* out of its Scripture context and read into it something not written in order to make Jesus our God. Concerning the words of this verse, the following is true.

   a. The verse does not read, "Before Abraham was made, I was <u>*the*</u> 'I AM.' "
   b. The verse speaks of the spiritual oneness of God's family or Elohim.
   c. The verse speaks of the prior existence of Jesus who was created first.
   d. Jesus' context is the prior phrase, "Abraham rejoiced to see my day."
   e. Jesus' context is also the prior phrase, "knowing and obeying God." V55
   f. The Jews misunderstood, thinking Jesus claimed he was God. He didn't.

Jesus said: "It is my FATHER that glorifieth me, of whom you say that he is your God. And you have not known HIM, but I know HIM. And if I shall say that I know HIM not, I shall be like to you, a liar. But I do know HIM, and do keep HIS word. Abraham your father rejoiced that he might see my day: he saw it, and was glad. The Jews therefore said to him: Thou art not yet fifty years old, and hast thou seen Abraham? Jesus said to them: Amen, amen I say to you, before Abraham was made, I am." John 8:54-58 (Douay-Rheims)

In the context of this teaching, Jesus asserts that he "knows God" and "keeps God's Word" [v55]. Then Jesus states after talking "about knowing God and keeping God's Word" that Abraham was glad to see "his" day [coming]. It is then that Jesus says he existed before Abraham. Trinity justifiers take this Scripture out of its context. Yet, within context, Jesus contrasts knowing his God to the fact the Jews didn't know HIM even thought they said they knew HIM. Ergo, the Jews lied about knowing God. These are the facts of this teaching. No amount of "reading into Scripture the trinity doctrine" can change the actual teachings of Jesus or the context of his teachings. The "I am" in this verse is not *the* "I AM" who spoke to Moses. Believing such dogma makes Jesus both a liar and an idiot.

5 Many read in Scripture where Jesus says to Paul, "Turn people from the power of Satan to that of God" and because of the trinity doctrine they think getting people to worship Jesus, as our God, is the answer. It isn't, because it denies what Jesus taught. It even denies what Apostle Peter taught about "turning people to God!"

Listen Again To Apostle Peter

"[Jesus] indeed was foreordained before the foundation of the world, but was manifest in these last times <u>for</u> you who through [Jesus] <u>believe in God</u>, who raised [Jesus] from the dead and gave [Jesus] glory, <u>so that your faith and hope are in God</u>." 1 Peter 1:21-22 (NKJV)

"For you <u>who</u> through Jesus <u>believe in God</u>,
So that your faith and hope are in God HIMSELF!"

Two Soul-Stealing Church Traditions

The above section contains two "soul-stealing" Church traditions. These are man-made doctrines, which negate one of God's Ten Commandments. In the first soul-stealing Church tradition, a money doctrine negated God's commandment to "honor your father and mother." In the second soul-stealing Church tradition, a worship doctrine negated God's second commandment to "not create any carved image or bow down to any carved image." The second worship doctrine has many Christians engaged in the idolatrous worship of an idol by bowing down to images of Jesus, Mary and Joseph.

The money doctrine is a covert means by which Satan can get people to serve money instead of God the FATHER. The carved image worship doctrine is a covert means by which Satan can get people into the idolatrous worship of a god of forgiveness called Jesus. Both doctrines are designed to take souls from God and shift them to Satan. Those who teach either of these soul-stealing doctrines are either woefully ignorant of Scripture, deceived by Satan or deceived by a long history of Church doctrinal programming, or are simply ministers of Satan. There is no other way that this Apostle of God can view such satanic "soul-stealing" teachings. Note that being "deceived" is another reason I've added to the prior list, but I highly doubt if the money grabbers are really deceived. The other smaller doctrine errors are designed to reinforce the larger ones, especially the false trinity doctrine. *Woe to those who lead God's people astray and into sin!*

If the trinity doctrine were true, the Church would not have 50% or more of Christians voting against God's interest. The fact that the Church is split means that at least half the people do not have God's Spirit and oneness. Yet, if the Church had not created the trinity apostasy, everyone in the Church would realize that without righteousness before God, there is no salvation and no amount of mouthing Jesus will make a difference. In truth, the 50% or more lost souls that attend Church regularly is a testimony to the effectiveness of Satan's trinity doctrine. Really, it's Satan's doctrine? Yes, do you think God would create a doctrine that makes liars out of both HIM and HIS begotten human Son Jesus?

The trinity doctrine was designed to come into its fullness in the 1960's after a long setup period so no one would make the connection to the Nicea 325 AD apostasy that started it all. Before 1965, Church teaching was basic. You needed to believe in God, Jesus, and to be a good person. Everyone knew Christians were different then. Christians would never have supported divorce, abortion and gay marriage. Yet, man's logic took Satan's trinity dogma to its logical next step. If it were true that God came down and died on the cross for us, then HE knew we couldn't help ourselves. If Jesus is truly our god of love and forgiveness, then anything goes. Ergo, whatever we do, we will be forgiven. Once saved always saved and even a second chance after one dies. Half of all Christians attending Church weekly now support evil in various forms. If the Church had done the work of Christ, this would not have occurred, as all believers would be of one mind, God's. The behavior of Christians today documents the effectiveness of the trinity doctrine lie.

Trinity Dogma © 2009 Rev. Edward G. Palmer

Lessons One Hundred Eight To One Hundred Sixty

108. Jesus taught in Matthew 15 that the Church negated God's commandment to "honor your father and mother."

109. The Church negated God's commandment to honor parents through a money doctrine that took all of the family's money so they could not help their parents.

110. In 2009, a similar money doctrine exists that perverts God's Word on tithing.

111. AFCM churches are the worst offenders of the modern Church money grab.

112. Other churches like the Assemblies of God use the modern money doctrine called tithing and even mainline churches like Lutheran have picked up the teaching.

113. The Catholic Church has deleted the second commandment from a theological practice. This commandment says, "Do not carve images or bow down to them."

114. The Catholic Church has split the ninth commandment on "do not covet" into two commandments and renumbered them nine and ten to make up for the deleted second commandment on "carved images and bowing down to them."

115. The Lutheran Church has the same Ten Commandments as the Catholic Church having deleted number two and split number nine to obtain a total of ten.

116. Fifty-five percent of bibles surveyed use the terminology of either "carved image" or "graven image" in God's second commandment. Forty-five percent of bibles surveyed use the terminology of "carved idols."

117. Older bibles generally refer to "carved image" or "graven image" in the second commandment of God.

118. Newer bibles generally refer to "carved idols" in the second commandment.

119. An exception to #117 is the James Moffatt Translation, which uses "idols."

120. An exception to #118 is the NET or New English Translation, which uses images.

121. The second commandment of God is missing in much of Catholic literature.

122. The second commandment of God is also missing in some Lutheran literature.

123. Martin Luther missed the deletion of the second commandment and the splitting of the ninth to make up a total of Ten Commandments.

124. The Catholic Church teaches idolatrous behavior by ignoring God's second commandment and encouraging the bowing down to a carved image [idol].

125. An outsider who attended Mass would observe an apostate service and seven distinct errors against God's commandments within Catholic churches.

126. God does not dwell in man-made structures such as church buildings.

127. God inhabits the praises of HIS people and seeks to dwell within our hearts.

128. Jesus taught that God's kingdom was "within us."
129. The Catholic Church deleted the second commandment to rationalize the use of images or icons to bow down to.
130. The Catholic Church rationalizes the renumbering of commandments because others do the same.
131. The Crucifix is the center worship image in Catholic Churches.
132. Statues or images of both Mary and Joseph usually accompany the Crucifix.
133. To know God, we must learn to be still and get into a quiet place with HIM.
134. Jesus taught us that God was "the FATHER" in John 20:17.
135. All bibles have 100% agreement on Jesus' teaching in John 20:17
136. Paul taught us the God was "the FATHER" in 1 Corinthians 8:6.
137. All bibles have 100% agreement on Paul's teaching in 1 Corinthians 8:6
138. Paul also taught that many people were unaware of who God was and who Jesus was in 1 Corinthians 8:7.
139. God has been clearly identified in Holy Scriptures as being the FATHER.
140. The God described by Jesus and Paul is the same God of the Old Testament.
141. The phrase "God the FATHER" is found repeatedly within Holy Scripture.
142. All Bible teachings about "God the FATHER" are consistent with the identity of God as disclosed by both Jesus and the Apostle Paul.
143. The phrase "God the Son" is unscriptural and not found in the Bible.
144. The phrase "God the Holy Spirit" is unscriptural and not found in the Bible.
145. The phrase "Mary Mother of God" is unscriptural and not found in the Bible.
146. If the doctrines reflected in #143-145 were true, God would have made sure that HIS Word reflected such attributes of HIS nature. It doesn't because they are false.
147. Scripture teaches that many people and groups of people actually knew that "the FATHER" is our God. The list includes Jesus, Paul, John, Peter, Jude, Timothy, Titus, James, Sylvanus, Thessalonians, Colossians, Ephesians, Philippians, Galatians, Corinthians, etc.
148. We see the list of #147 shown in the Scripture citations of "God the FATHER."
149. Jesus taught Paul to "open peoples eyes" and to "turn them to God."
150. James confirms that the objective of Jesus was to "turn people to God."
151. People use the trinity doctrine to interpret Scripture.
152. Using the trinity doctrine to interpret Scripture distorts its meaning. This is especially true when it comes to the nature of God and the teachings of HIS son.
153. Jesus taught about the oneness of God's Spirit with all who belong to God. Ergo, every true believer has God inside and can truly say, "I and the FATHER are one."

154. A true salvation teaching reflects both repentance and a return to God.

155. The New Testament cannot be understood without first understanding the Old Testament.

156. Jesus fulfilled the Law of God and did not delete one "tittle" of it.

157. The doctrine of the money-grab is a covert means of Satan designed to take souls away from God through a shift of focus to worldly things. You cannot be friends of the world without becoming an enemy of God.

158. The doctrine of the carved-image is a covert means of Satan designed to take souls away from God through a shift of focus to idolatrous worship of a new "god of love" called Jesus. It uses images and a bowing down process that were strictly forbidden by God's second commandment. It substitutes God's Son in place of the FATHER, which Jesus and Paul identified for us as being our only "God."

159. The behavior of Christians today demonstrate the effectiveness of the trinity doctrine lie as 50% or more no longer support God's righteousness and are clearly headed to Hell because they are lawless people in the eyes of God and HIS Son.

160. Scripture doesn't teach a trinity doctrine. The Church *created* a trinity doctrine at the council of Nicea in 325 AD.

The Apostles' Creed (Circa 150 AD)

We believe in God, the FATHER Almighty
    Creator of Heaven and earth.

We believe in Jesus Christ, HIS only Son, our Lord.
    He was conceived by the power of the Holy Spirit
        And born of the Virgin Mary
    He suffered under Pontius Pilate,
        Was crucified, died, and was buried.
    He descended to the dead.
    On the third day he arose again.
    He ascended into Heaven,
        And is seated at the right hand of the FATHER.
    He will come again to judge the living and the dead.

We believe in the Holy Spirit,
    The holy Catholic Church,
    The communion of Saints,
    The forgiveness of sins,
    The resurrection of the body,
    And the life everlasting. Amen

Catholic <u>Apostles' Creed</u> as found in (2002), *RitualSong, A Hymnal and Service Book for Roman Catholics,* p296, GIA Publications, Inc., Chicago.

Origin of Apostles' Creed

"The Apostles' Creed is referenced in many ancient documents. It is quoted in various versions by Irenaeus, Tertullian, Novatian, Marcellus, Rufinus, Ambrose, Augustine, Nicetus, and Eusebius Gallus. *In Eusebius's historical writings, he claims the Nicene Creed derived its basis from the Apostles' Creed. It is explained in Cyril of Jerusalem's famous 34 catechetical lectures (ca. 347 AD).*" Source: *Wikipedia Apostles' Creed data.*

Comments on Apostles' Creed

While Eusebius's writings in 347 AD state that the Nicene Creed was derived from the Apostles' Creed, others claim just the opposite occurred and that the Apostles' Creed surfaced later than the Nicene Creed. Still others firmly believe that the Apostles' Creed was the work of the original twelve apostles [disciples] of Jesus Christ.

This I know, there is no deliberate apostasy built into the Apostles' Creed and major apostasy built into subsequent Church creeds. The one line I do question is the one that reads, "He descended to the dead." Some versions of this creed read, "He descended to Hell." The statement comes from a misread of Ephesians 4:9. The Bible and this verse in Ephesians teach that Christ ascended, but first descended from Heaven to the earth.

On the cross, Jesus told the thief that "this day" he would be with Christ in Paradise.

> **[Jesus] replied to him [the thief], "Amen, I say to you, today you will be with me in Paradise." Luke 23:43 (NAB)**

So, the phrase "to the dead" is correct as in "going to visit with the dead [souls]." I don't know, but I think Paradise might be up vs. down. Therefore, at this time, Scripture only teaches, "He visited the dead in Paradise." In the Book of Enoch we read the following text, which helps to explain the Paradise concept. Understand that Paradise is not Heaven.

> **"From thence I [Enoch] proceeded to another spot, where I saw on the west a great and lofty mountain, a strong rock, and four delightful places. Internally it was deep, capacious, and very smooth; as smooth as if it had been rolled over: It was both deep and dark to behold. Then Raphael, one of the holy angels who were with me, answered and said, 'these are the delightful places where the spirits, the souls of the dead, will be collected; for them they were formed; and here will be collected all the souls of the sons [and daughters] of men. These places, in which they dwell, shall they occupy until the Day of Judgment, and until their appointed period' " Enoch XXII [V]: 1-4.**

The Book of Enoch was excised from Scripture, but Ethiopian copies were found and now the teaching is readily available on the Internet. I have studied Enoch and believe it is truly God's Word that Enoch relates to us. So Paradise would be the place where the souls of men and women are collected and await God's judgment, which Christ will execute. Remember the prior teaching of Christ about those who know Yahweh and obey His teachings? Remember they bypass judgment? I believe they also bypass Paradise.

The Apostles' Creed Beliefs

1) **We believe in God, the FATHER Almighty**, which is what Christ and Paul taught.

2) **We believe in Jesus Christ, HIS only Son, our Lord.**

> *Note: the phrase "only Son" is a misnomer in that there are many sons and daughters of God, but there is only one human begotten Son of God, Jesus Christ. This line would have more Scripture support if it read, "We believe in Jesus Christ, God's only human begotten Son, our Lord."*

3) **We believe in the Holy Spirit.**

Everything else in the Apostles' Creed under the above three main headings are accurate Scripture teachings. The issues of "descending" and "only Son" would more accurately reflect Scripture if updated. However, these are theological nuances and not deliberately "built-in" apostate teachings. Go ahead and use the Apostles' Creed. I have no problem reciting the above creed wording, but I do offer a Scripture update on the next page.

What the Apostles' Creed Does Not Ask

The Apostles' Creed does not ask that you believe Jesus is God or that the Holy Spirit is God. Nor does it ask you to believe they are coequal with the FATHER. To do so, like other creeds, literally makes Jesus Christ a liar when he said, "The FATHER is greater than I."

> **Jesus said: "You heard me tell you, 'I am going away and I will come back to you.' If you loved me, you would rejoice that I am going to the FATHER; for the FATHER is greater than I." John 14:28 (NAB)**

Jesus said: "The FATHER is greater than I [am]!"

This is just one example of an unequal statement from the teachings of Jesus concerning the God that he served. So, I ask this trinity doctrine question again, "Is Jesus a liar?" If not, then why does any Church doctrine make him out to be one? Verily I say unto you that God will repay with a vengeance all whose teachings or doctrines, in effect, turns the words of our Lord Jesus Christ into a lie. By doing so, they blaspheme God, whose very words our Lord Jesus communicated to us as a prophet. Therefore, to deny Christ's words is to deny God's very OWN instructions given to mankind. Ergo, no doctrinal creed based upon God's Holy Word would deny what HIS Scripture teaches or would deny the words that HE HIMSELF gave Jesus. Learn this lesson well right now concerning Jesus …

The teachings of Jesus are immutable, irreformable, infallible, indefectible and indestructible!

Trinity Dogma © 2009 Rev. Edward G. Palmer

The Apostles' Creed (2009 AD)

We believe in God, the FATHER Almighty
    Creator of Heaven and earth.

We believe in Jesus Christ, <u>God's only human begotten Son</u>, our Lord.
    He was conceived by the power of the Holy Spirit
        And born of the Virgin Mary
    He suffered under Pontius Pilate,
        Was crucified, died, and was buried.
    <u>He visited the dead in Paradise.</u>
    On the third day he arose again.
    He ascended into Heaven,
        And is seated at the right hand of the FATHER.
    He will come again to judge the living and the dead.

We believe in the Holy Spirit,
    The holy Catholic Church,
    The communion of Saints,
    The forgiveness of sins,
    The resurrection of the body,
    And the life everlasting. Amen

> Jesus said to her, "Go to my brothers!" John 20:17 (NAB) "Concerning HIS Son [Jesus], who was made to [Joseph] of the seed of David, <u>according to the flesh</u>." Romans 1:3 And, also see <u>made like us</u> in Heb 2:17. (Douay-

> [Jesus] replied to him [the thief], "Amen, I say to you, today you will be with me in Paradise." Luke 23:43 (NAB)

Apostle Edward's 04/14/09 update. Note: The words "holy Catholic Church" means "God's holy <u>universal</u> Church." There is only one Church and it is not composed of various denominations. Instead, the Church is a collection of souls, [individuals] committed to doing the will and work of God [FATHER] on earth.

Christ warns us to do God's will!

Jesus said, "Not everyone who says to me, 'Lord, Lord,' will enter the kingdom of Heaven, but only the one who does the will of my FATHER in Heaven." Matthew 7:21 (NAB)

It is not God's will for the Church to lie about HIS nature or the nature of HIS only human begotten Son, Jesus Christ!

Those in the Church who do so are excluded!

Trinity Dogma © 2009 Rev. Edward G. Palmer

The Roman Pantheon
Sixty-Four Identified Roman Pagan Gods

Prior to the decision of Nicea in 325 AD that defined and adopted the Trinity [the triune Christian god] — there was a history of Romans worshipping hundreds of pagan gods. These sixty-four pagan gods are some of those that the superstitious Romans worshipped.

#	Roman Pagan God	Origin (If known)	Characteristics
1	Annona		Mythical personification of the annual food supply
2	Apollo	Greek	God of healing and prophecy
3	Asclepius	Greek	God of healing
4	Attis	Phrygian	Beloved of Cybele
5	Bacchus	Greek Dionysos	God of wine
6	Bellona		Goddess of war
7	Bona Dea		The 'Good Goddess' unnamed spirit whose rites were attended only by women
8	Cardea		Household goddess of door hinges
9	Castor & Pollus (Dioscuri)	Greek	Two legendary heroes
10	Ceres	Greek Demeter	Goddess of agriculture
11	Consus		God of the granary
12	Cybele	Phrygian	See 'Magna Mater'
13	Diana	Greek Artemis	Goddess of light, also unity of peoples
14	Dis	Greek Pluto	God of the underworld
15	Faunus	Greek Pan	God of fertility
16	Flora		Goddess of fertility and flowers
17	Forculus		Household god of doors
18	Fortuna (or Fors, Fors Fortuna)		Goddess of good luck
19	Genius		Male spirit of the Roman family
20	Glaucus		A sea god
21	Hercules	Greek Herakles	God of victory and commercial enterprise
22	Hermes		See Mercury
23	Isis	Egyptian	Goddess of the earth
24	Janus		God of doorways
25	Juno	Greek Hera	Goddess of women
26	Jupiter *(English Jove)*	Greek Zeus	God of the heavens
27	Juturna		Goddess of fountains
28	Lar (plural Lares)		A spirit of the household

Trinity Dogma © 2009 Rev. Edward G. Palmer

The Roman Pantheon Con't

29	Larvae (or Lemures)		Mischievous spirits of the dead
30	Liber		God of fertility and vine growing
31	Libitina		Goddess of the dead
32	Limentinus		Household god of the threshold
33	Magna Mater	Phrygian Cybele	The 'Great Mother' goddess of nature
34	Magnes		Spirits of the dead
35	Mars		God of war
36	Mercury	Greek Hermes	God of merchants
37	Minerva	Greek Athena	Goddess of crafts and industry
38	Mithras	Persian Mithra	God of the sun
39	Neptune	Greek Poseidon	God of the sea
40	Nundina		Presiding Goddess at the purification and naming of children
41	Ops		God of the wealth of the harvest
42	Osiris	Egyptian	Consort of Iris
43	Pales		God/Goddess of the shepherd
44	Penates		Household spirits of the store cupboard
45	Picumnus & Pilumnus		Agricultural gods associated with childbirth
46	Pomona		Goddess of fruit
47	Portunus		God of harbors
48	Priapus		God of fertility in gardens and flocks
49	Quirinus		State god under whose name Romulus was worshipped
50	Robigus		God of mildew
51	Roma		Goddess of Rome
52	Sabazius	Phrygian	God of vegetation
53	Salus		God of health
54	Serapis	Egyptian	God of the sky
55	Saturn	Greek Chronos	God of Sowing
56	Silvanus		God of woods and fields
57	Sol	Helios	God of the sun
58	Tellus		Goddess of earth
59	Terminus		God of property boundaries
60	Venus	Greek Aphrodite	Goddess of love
61	Vertumnus (Vortumnus)		God of orchards
62	Vesta	Greek Hestia	Goddess of the hearth
63	Volturnus		God of the Tiber river
64	Vulcan	Greek Hephaistos	God of fire

SOURCE: www.roman-empire.net/religion/pantheon.html 04/14/09

Roman Pantheon Summary

"The Romans believed in many different gods and goddesses. For everything imaginable they had a god or goddess in charge. Mars for example was the god of war. This meant he was good at fighting and it meant that he had most of all the soldiers at heart. A Roman soldier would hence most likely pray to Mars for strength in battle. But Minerva was the goddess of wisdom, intelligence and learning. Not many soldiers would ask her for help. But perhaps a schoolboy would ask her to help him learn his grammar or understand his math better! Or the emperor would ask her to give him wisdom so that he might rule the country wisely. And so, the Romans indeed had hundreds of different gods. This entire collection of all their gods was called the **Pantheon**." SOURCE: www.roman-empire.net

A Summary of Roman History

This section contains excerpts taken from material found at the www.roman-empire.net web site. Bracketed words indicate sentences with minor editing for the ease of reading. To understand the trinity doctrine and its creation, you must also understand the context in which the trinity was created. That context includes the combination of all the Roman pagan gods worshipped, the political environment of the Roman Empire, and also Constantine's desire for religious peace and unity within his empire. Apostle Edward

"If anything, the Romans had a practical attitude to religion, as to most things, which perhaps explains why they themselves had difficulty in taking to the idea of a single, all-seeing, all-powerful god. In so far as the Romans had a religion of their own, it was not based on any central belief, but on a mixture of fragmented rituals, taboos, superstitions, and traditions, which they collected over the years from a number of sources. To the Romans, religion was less a spiritual experience than a contractual relationship between mankind and the forces, which were believed to control people's existence and well-being. The result of such religious attitudes were two things: a state cult, the significant influence on political and military events of which outlasted the republic, and a private concern, in which the head of the family oversaw the domestic rituals and prayers in the same way as the representatives of the people performed the public ceremonials."

"However, as circumstances and people's view of the world changed, individuals whose personal religious needs remained unsatisfied turned increasingly during the first century AD to the mysteries, which were of Greek origin, and to the cults of the east."

"Most of the Roman gods and goddesses were a blend of several religious influences. Many were introduced via the Greek colonies of southern Italy. Many also had their roots in old religions of the Etruscans or Latin tribes. Often the old Etruscan or Latin name survived but the deity over time became to be seen as the Greek god of equivalent or similar nature. And so it is that the Greek and Roman pantheon look very similar, but for different names."

Romans had difficulty believing in a single all-powerful god!

"Most [Roman] form of religious activity required some kind of sacrifice. And prayer could be a confusing matter due to some gods having multiple names or their sex even being unknown. The practice of Roman religion was a confusing thing.

The Roman was by nature a very superstitious person. Emperors would tremble and even legions refuse to march if the omens were bad ones.

If the Roman state entertained temples and rituals for the benefit of the greater gods, then the Romans in the privacy of their own homes also worshipped their domestic deities. To the Roman peasant the world around simply abounded with gods, spirits and omens. A multitude of festivals were held to appease the gods."

Romans worshipped many gods, spirits and omens!

The Beginnings of Christianity

"The beginnings of Christianity are very blurry, as far as historical fact is concerned. The birth date of Jesus himself is uncertain. (The idea of Jesus birth being the year **AD 1**, is due rather to a judgment made some 500 years after the event took place.) Many point to the year **4 BC** as the most likely date for Christ's birth, and yet that remains very uncertain. The year of his death is also not clearly established. It is assumed it took place between **AD 26** and **AD 36** (most likely though between AD 30 and AD 36), during the reign of Pontius Pilate as prefect of Judea. Historically speaking, Jesus of Nazareth was a charismatic Jewish leader, exorcist and religious teacher. To the Christians however he is the Messiah, the human personification of God. Evidence of Jesus' life and effect in Palestine is very patchy. He was clearly not one of the militant Jewish zealots, and yet eventually the Roman rulers did perceive him as a security risk.

Roman power appointed the priests who were in charge of the religious sites of Palestine. And, Jesus openly denounced these priests. [This] much is known. This indirect threat to Roman power, together with the Roman perception that Jesus was claiming to be the 'King of the Jews,' was the reason for his condemnation. The Roman apparatus saw itself merely dealing with a minor problem which otherwise might have grown into a greater threat to their authority. So in essence, the reason for Jesus' crucifixion was politically motivated. However, his death was hardly noticed by Roman historians.

Jesus' death [would] have dealt a fatal blow to the memory of his teachings, were it not for the determination of his followers. The most effective of these followers in spreading the new religious teachings was Paul of Tarsus, generally known as Saint Paul. St Paul, who held Roman citizenship, is famed for his missionary voyages, which took him from Palestine into the empire (Syria, Turkey, Greece and Italy) to spread his new religion to the non-Jews (for until then Christianity was generally understood to be a Jewish sect).

[The] actual definite outlines of the new [Christian] religion of that day [are] largely unknown. Naturally, the general Christian ideals [would] have been preached, but few scriptures [were readily] available."

Rome's Relationship with the early Christians

"The Roman authorities hesitated for a long time over how to deal with this new cult. They largely appreciated this new religion as subversive and potentially dangerous. For Christianity, with its insistence on only one god, seemed to threaten the principle of religious toleration, which had guaranteed (religious) peace for so long among the people of the empire. Most of all Christianity clashed with the official state religion of the empire, for Christians refused to perform Caesar worship. This, in the Roman mindset, demonstrated their disloyalty to their rulers.

Persecution of the Christians began with Nero's bloody repression of **AD 64.** This was only a rash and sporadic repression though it is perhaps the one that remains the most infamous of them all.

The first real recognition [of] Christianity other than Nero's slaughter was an inquiry by emperor Domitian who supposedly, upon hearing that the Christians refused to perform Caesar worship, sent investigators to Galilee to inquire on his family, about fifty years after the crucifixion [circa **AD 83**]. They found some poor smallholders [people having a small piece of land], including the great-nephew of Jesus, interrogated them and then released them without charge. The fact, however, that the Roman emperor should take interest in this sect proves that by this time the Christians no longer merely represented an obscure little sect.

Towards the end of the first century [circa **AD 100**] the Christians appeared to sever all their ties with the Judaism and established itself independently. Though with this separation form Judaism, Christianity emerged as a largely unknown religion to the Roman authorities. And Roman ignorance of this new cult bred suspicion. Rumors were abounding about secretive Christian rituals; rumors of child sacrifice, incest and cannibalism. Major revolts of the Jews in Judea in the early second century led to great resentment of the Jews and of the Christians, who were still largely understood by the Romans to be a Jewish sect. The repressions, which followed for both Christians and Jews, were severe.

Christians severed ties with Judaism and grew independently!

During the second century AD, Christians were persecuted for their beliefs largely because these did not allow them to give the statutory reverence to the images of the gods and of the emperor. Also their act of worship transgressed the edict of Trajan, forbidding meetings of secret societies. To the government, it was civil disobedience. The Christians themselves meanwhile thought such edicts suppressed their freedom of worship. However, despite such differences, with emperor Trajan a period of toleration appeared to set in."

Christians were persecuted for failing to give statutory reverence to images of the Roman gods and the Roman emperor!

"Pliny the Younger, as governor of Nithynia in **AD 111**, was so exercised by the troubles with the Christians that he wrote to Trajan asking for guidance on how to deal with them. Trajan, displaying considerable wisdom, replied:

' The actions you have taken, my dear Pliny, in investigating the cases of those brought before you as Christians, are correct. It is impossible to lay down a general rule, which can apply to particular cases. Do not go looking for Christians. If they are brought before you and the charge is proven, they must be punished, provided that if someone denies they are Christian and gives proof of it, by offering reverence to our gods, they shall be acquitted on the grounds of repentance even if they have previously incurred suspicion. Anonymous written accusations shall be disregarded as evidence. They set a bad example which is contrary to the spirit of our times.'

Christians were not actively sought out by [the] network of [Roman] spies. Under his successor Hadrian [this] policy seemed to continue. Also the fact that Hadrian actively persecuted the Jews, but not the Christians shows that by that time the Romans were drawing a clear distinction between the two religions.

Romans started making a distinction between Christians and Jews!

The great persecutions of **AD 165-180** under Marcus Aurelius included the terrible acts committed upon the Christians of Lyons in **AD 177**. This period, far more than Nero's earlier rage [] defined the Christian understanding of martyrdom. Christianity is often portrayed as the religion of the poor and the slaves. This is not necessarily a true picture. From the beginning there appeared to have been wealthy and influential figures who at least sympathized with the Christians, even members of court. And it appeared that Christianity maintained its appeal to such highly connected persons. Marcia, the concubine of the emperor Commodus, for example, used her influence to achieve the release of Christian prisoners from the mines."

The Great Persecution - AD 303

Christianity [had] generally grown and established some roots across the empire in the years following the persecution by Marcus Aurelius. Then it had especially prospered from about **AD 260** onwards enjoying widespread toleration by the Roman authorities. But with the reign of Diocletian things would change. Towards the end of his long reign, Diocletian became ever more concerned about the high positions held by many Christians in Roman society and, particularly, the army. On a visit to the Oracle of Apollo at Didyma near Miletus, he was advised by the pagan oracle to halt the rise of the Christians. And so on 23 February **AD 303**, on the Roman day of the gods of boundaries, the *terminalia*, Diocletian enacted what was to become perhaps the greatest persecution of Christians under Roman rule. Diocletian and, perhaps all the more viciously, his Caesar Galerius launched a serious purge against the sect which they saw as becoming far too powerful and hence, too dangerous. In Rome, Syria, Egypt and Asia Minor (Turkey) the Christians suffered most. However, in the west, beyond the immediate grasp of the two persecutors things were far less ferocious."

Constantine the Great - Christianization of the Empire

"The key moment in the establishment [of] Christianity as the predominant religion of the Roman empire, happened in **AD 312** when emperor Constantine on the eve before battle against the rival emperor Maxentius had a vision of the sign of Christ (the so called *chi-rho* symbol) in a dream. And Constantine was to have the symbol inscribed on his helmet and ordered all his soldiers (or at least those of his bodyguard) to [put] it on their shields. It was after the crushing victory he inflicted on his opponent against overwhelming odds that Constantine declared he owed his victory to the god of the Christians.

> **However, Constantine's claim to conversion is not without controversy. There are many who see in his conversion [] the political realization of the potential power of Christianity instead of any celestial vision [of his].**

Constantine had inherited a very tolerant attitude towards Christians from his father, but for the years of his rule previous to that fateful night in **AD 312** there was no definite indication of any gradual conversion towards the Christian faith. Although he did already have Christian bishops in his royal entourage before AD 312. But however truthful his conversion might have been, it [still would] change the fate of Christianity for good.

In meetings with his rival emperor Licinius, Constantine secured religious tolerance towards Christians all over the empire. Until **AD 324** Constantine appeared to on purposely blur the distinction of which god it was he followed, the Christian god or pagan sun god Sol. Perhaps at this time he truly hadn't made up his mind yet. Perhaps it was just that he felt his power was not yet established enough to confront the pagan majority of the empire with a Christian ruler. However, substantial gestures were made toward the Christians very soon after the fateful Battle of the Milvian Bridge in **AD 312**. Already in **AD 313** tax exemptions were granted to Christian clergy and money was granted to rebuild the major churches in Rome. Also in **AD 314** Constantine already engaged in a major meeting of bishops at Milan to deal with problems befalling the church in the 'Donatist schism'. [A political dispute that originated in the Church of Carthage].

Constantine worked to consolidate Roman political power!

But once Constantine had defeated his last rival emperor Licinius in **AD 324**, the last of Constantine's restraint disappeared and a Christian emperor (or at least one who championed the Christian cause) ruled over the entire empire. He built a vast new basilica church on the Vatican hill, where reputedly St Peter had been martyred. Other great churches were built by Constantine, such as the great St John Lateran in Rome or the reconstruction of the great church of Nicomedia, which had been destroyed by Diocletian."

After defeating his last rival, Constantine ruled as a Christian emperor!
Constantine built great Christian churches, including the Basilica on Vatican hill!

Trinity Dogma © 2009 Rev. Edward G. Palmer

After consolidating all political power,
Constantine became hostile towards pagan gods!

"Apart from building great monuments to Christianity, Constantine now also became openly hostile toward the pagans. Even pagan sacrifice itself was forbidden. Pagan temples (except those of the previous official Roman state cult) had their treasures confiscated. These treasures were largely given to the Christian churches instead. Some cults which were deemed sexually immoral by Christian standards were forbidden and their temples were razed. Gruesomely brutal laws were introduced to enforce Christian sexual morality. Constantine was evidently not an emperor who had decided to gradually educate the people of his empire [about] this new religion. Far more, the empire was shocked into a new [Christian] religious order."

Constantine forced the Roman Empire into accepting
his newly adopted Christian religious order!

Church Fights Dissent

"But in the same year as Constantine achieved supremacy over the empire (and effectively over the Christian church) the Christian faith itself suffered a grave crisis. Arianism, a heresy that challenged the church's view of God (the father) and Jesus (the son), was creating a serious divide in the church."

Note: By this time, the Church was split between the teachings of Arius that God was only the FATHER and Athanasius who taught a Trinitarian view of God. This was no longer about Scripture, but about politics in the Roman Empire. Arius, on his part, refused to accept the apostasy of the trinity teaching. Complete information on Arius is available on the Internet. Heresy is anything opposing the Roman Catholic Church.

Constantine Convenes Council Of Nicea

"Constantine called the famous [**AD 325**] Council of Nicea, which decided the definition of the Christian deity as the Holy Trinity, God the father, God the son and God the Holy Spirit. Christianity previously [had] been unclear about its [god] message [but] then the Council of Nicea (together with a later council at Constantinople in **381 AD**) created a clearly defined core belief."

God did not divinely reveal the trinity doctrine!
Men created it at the Council of Nicea!

"However, the nature of its creation - a council - and the diplomatically sensitive way in defining the [trinity] formula, to many suggest the creed of the Holy Trinity to be rather a political construct between theologians and politicians rather than anything achieved by divine inspiration. It is hence often sought that the Council of Nicea [**AD 325**] represents the Christian church becoming a more worldly institution, moving away from its innocent beginnings in its ascent to power."

Trinity Dogma © 2009 Rev. Edward G. Palmer

"The Christian church continued to grow and rise in importance under Constantine. Within his reign the cost of the church already became larger than the cost of the entire imperial civil service. As for emperor Constantine; he bowed out in the same fashion in which he had lived, leaving it still unclear to historians today, if he truly had completely converted to Christianity, or not. He was baptized on his deathbed. It was not an unusual practice for Christians of the day to leave their baptism for such a time. However, it still fails to answer completely to what point this was due to conviction and not for political purposes, considering the succession of his sons."

Christian Heresy

"One of the primary problems of early Christianity was that of heresy. Heresy [is] defined as [any] departure from the traditional [Orthodox Trinitarian] Christian beliefs [or] the creation of new ideas, rituals and forms of worship within the Christian church. *This was especially dangerous to a faith in which for a long time the rules as to what was the proper Christian belief remained very vague and open to interpretation.* The result of [a charge] of heresy was often [a] bloody slaughter. Religious suppression against heretics became to any account just as brutal as some of the excesses of Roman emperors in suppressing the Christians."

A Church heresy charge often resulted in a bloody slaughter!

Julian the Apostate

"If Constantine's conversion of the empire had been harsh, it was irreversible. When in **AD 361** Julian ascended to the throne and officially renounced Christianity, he could do little to change the religious make-up of an empire in which Christianity by then dominated. [That's because] under Constantine and his sons, being a Christian [was] almost a pre-requisite for receiving any official position, [and by then] the entire working of the empire had been turned over to Christians.

It is unclear to what point the population had converted to Christianity (though the numbers [were] rising quickly), but it is clear that the institutions of empire must by the time Julian came to power have been dominated by Christians. Hence a reverse was impossible, unless a pagan emperor of the drive and ruthlessness of Constantine would have emerged. Julian the Apostate was no such man. Far more does history paint him as a gentle intellectual, who simply tolerated Christianity in spite of his disagreement with it. Christian teachers lost their jobs, as Julian argued that it made little sense for them to teach pagan texts of which they did not approve.

Also some of the financial privileges, which the church had enjoyed, were now refused. But by no means could this have been seen as a renewal of Christian persecution. In fact, in the east [side] of the empire, Christian mobs ran riot and vandalized the pagan temples, which Julian had re-instated. Julian [was] not a violent man of the likes of Constantine, [because] his response to Christian outrages [was] never felt, [and he] died in **AD 363**. If his reign had a been a brief setback for Christianity, it had only provided further proof that Christianity was here to stay."

The Power of the Church

With the death of Julian the Apostate matters quickly returned to normal for the Christian church as it resumed its role as the religion of the power. In **AD 380** emperor Theodosius took the final step and made Christianity the official religion of state.

Severe punishments were introduced for people who disagreed with the official version of Christianity. Furthermore, becoming a member of the clergy became a possible career for the educated classes, for the bishops were gaining ever more influence. At the great council of Constantinople a further decision was reached which placed the bishopric of Rome above that of Constantinople. This in effect confirmed the church's more political outlook, as until [then] the prestige of the bishoprics had been ranked according to the church's apostolic history. And [at] that particular time, preference for the bishop of Rome evidently appeared to be greater than for the bishop of Constantinople.

In **AD 390** alas a massacre in Thessalonica revealed the new order to the world. After a massacre of some seven thousand people the emperor Theodosius was excommunicated and required to do penance for this crime. This did not mean that now the church was the highest authority in the empire, but it proved that now the church felt sufficiently confident to challenge the emperor himself on matters of moral authority."

> *"Severe punishments were introduced for people who disagreed with the 'official' version of Christianity!"*

SOURCE: www.roman-empire.net/religion/religion.html 04/14/09

The Trinity Doctrine Was Not Created In A Vacuum!

There was a societal context and no divine revelation from anyone in any moment of time! The trinity doctrine was developed and word-smithed by humans at Nicea in 325AD.

The above summary of Roman history helps explain the context in which the trinity doctrine was developed. There was a pagan god context, a Roman political context and a Christian belief context. With hundreds of pagan gods being worshipped, the division in Christian beliefs and the need for political unity, it was Constantine who drove the creation and adoption of the trinity at the council of Nicea in AD 325. Constantine had already conquered his enemies and now saw the need for uniting his empire. The trinity was the solution created to unite religious beliefs in the Roman Empire, by force of course!

Once again God has altered the words I write for HIM with HIS Word. So, I will give you exactly what God has just given me at 1:35 pm on April 16, 2009 from HIS Word. It is not God who shuts down the debate and discussion on any subject. In fact, you can go to God with any of your concerns. Just like Jesus has taught. "Go directly to God." Our FATHER makes this clear in HIS Word. And, if you come to HIM with a sincere heart, you will get answers to your petitions. Remember to ask in Jesus' name!

God said: "Come now, and let us reason together." Isaiah 1:18 (NKJV)

So, in history, it is self-evident that the council of Nicea created a dogma, removed all discussion about the dogma, and then persecuted and even killed anyone who opposed the dogma! Does this sound like anything that would come from God? The God who respects your free will? Even today, such persecution continues within Christianity. Not only would God not shut down your discussion, HE would also not contradict the truth found in HIS Holy Scripture! Ergo, the trinity is not of God, because it contradicts God.

Twenty-Two Lessons From Roman History

1. People in the Roman Empire worshipped hundreds of pagan gods.
2. The hundreds of pagan gods worshipped were collectively called the Pantheon.
3. Pagan gods were assigned to everything in human life, even "door hinges."
4. People in the Roman Empire were very superstitious people.
5. People in the Roman Empire had difficulty believing in a single all-powerful god.
6. Christianity's trinity began in the context of hundreds of pagan gods.
7. Christianity's trinity began in the context of a political environment.
8. Christianity's trinity began in the context of a split Christian Church.
9. Roman authorities were wary of Christians and the power they could accumulate.
10. Eventually Christianity broke away from Judaism and became independent.
11. Eventually the Romans treated Christians differently than Jews.
12. Christians were persecuted for not giving reverence to images of Roman gods.
13. Christians were persecuted for not giving reverence to images of the Emperor.
14. There were deadly persecutions of Christians by Roman Emperors.
15. Constantine won a great battle and gave credit to the god of the Christians.
16. Constantine promoted Christianity cautiously at first due to political concerns.
17. After consolidating political power, Constantine ruled as a Christian emperor.
18. Constantine's conversion to Christianity was questioned due to the political nature of his religious acts and the diplomacy he displayed at Nicea in AD 325 to get a unified agreement on the Trinity definition of the god of the Christians.

19. After the Nicea trinity decision, the Church fought any dissent from its orthodox teachings. They punished dissent, persecuted those with other opinions and even slaughtered those who held other beliefs other than the trinity.

20. Arius and others dissented from the Nicea trinity decision and claimed it was apostasy and did not represent the God the apostles taught.

21. The trinity decision was a political unity decision of Constantine to refocus the Roman Empire away from hundreds of pagan gods onto just a single triune god.

22. Constantine forcibly imposed the new Christian trinity god on the Roman Empire and became hostile to all other gods.

Constantine converts to Arianism On his deathbed in AD 337!

"Constantine had known death would soon come. Within the Church of the Holy Apostles, Constantine had secretly prepared a final resting-place for himself. It came sooner than he had expected. Soon after the Feast of Easter **AD 337**, Constantine fell seriously ill. He left Constantinople for the hot baths near his mother's city of Helenopolis (Altinova), on the southern shores of the Gulf of Izmit. There, in a church his mother built in honor of Lucian the Apostle, he prayed, and there he realized that he was dying. Seeking purification, he became a catechumen, and attempted a return to Constantinople, making it only as far as a suburb of Nicomedia. He summoned the bishops, and told them of his hope to be baptized in the River Jordan, where Christ was written to have been baptized. He requested the baptism right away, promising to live a more Christian life should he live through his illness. The bishops, Eusebius records, 'performed the sacred ceremonies according to custom.' **He chose the Arianizing bishop Eusebius of Nicomedia, bishop of the city where he lay dying, as his baptizer.** In postponing his baptism, he followed one custom at the time, which postponed baptism until old age or death. It was thought Constantine put off baptism as long as he did so as to be absolved from as much of his sin as possible. Constantine died soon after at a suburban villa called Achyron, on the last day of the fifty-day festival of Pentecost directly following Easter, on 22 May 337."

SOURCE: http://en.wikipedia.org/wiki/Constantine_I#Sickness_and_death 04/16/09

Constantine's deathbed conversion by an Arian Priest was a renunciation of the trinity doctrine that he forced upon the Roman Empire via the Council of Nicea in **AD 325**. Constantine recognized that YAHWEH was not a triune god. Ergo, the very creator of the trinity doctrine recognized his political work on his deathbed. This is fact as, "Arianizing bishop Eusebius" would not have asked him to accept a false god. It was in **AD 381** at the First Council of Constantinople that the Church made Arianism a heresy and crime and sought to completely destroy it. Arianism is reported to have been a force in Europe for about 267 years (**319 - 586 AD**) until the Roman Catholic Church drove it underground.

There are those who write the opposite of this history claiming that Constantine was all along an Arian believer. This is revisionist history. A letter from Constantine to Arius in **AD 333** only four years before his death indicates Constantine thought Arius to be a mad man, but was "as a man of God" willing to listen to Arius' thinking. Since Constantine called forth the Council of Nicea, adopted the trinity dogma, and then only on his deathbed converted to Arianism, the facts speak for themselves. Constantine made a political move to consolidate "gods" in the Roman Empire. By the time of his death, he had realized that he made a terrible mistake in promoting the trinity god concept.

After **AD 381**, in order to consolidate Church control over Christian doctrine, the Church confiscated all written works that opposed its "orthodox" teachings. It also made it a crime to teach anything other than orthodoxy [what the Roman Catholic Church taught]. It has been reported that as many as 300 gospels may have existed in the early days. The Roman Catholic Church selected four and destroyed all of the other gospels. Attempts to destroy all other opposing manuscripts met with only limited success. Writings such as the *Book of Enoch* and others have surfaced from Ethiopian Christians and other sources like the *Dead Sea Scrolls* and the *Nag Hammadi Library*. As a result, many manuscripts are now translated and available on the Internet for research. Ergo, if you search for the "Gospel of Thomas," "Gospel of Phillip," and many other ancient documents, you will be surprised at what you will find available in spite of Church efforts to destroy manuscripts.

God will protect HIS Holy Scriptures!

Tertullian Coins "Trinity"

"Hints of Trinitarian beliefs can also be seen in the teachings of extra-biblical writers as early as the end of the first century. However, the clearest early expression of the concept came with Tertullian, a Latin theologian who wrote in the early third century (**AD 213**). Tertullian coined the words "Trinity" and "person" and explained that the Father, Son and Holy Spirit were "one in essence - not one in Person.

About a century later, in **AD 325**, the Council of Nicea set out to officially define the relationship of the Son to the Father, in response to the controversial teachings of Arius. Led by bishop Athanasius, the council established the doctrine of the Trinity as orthodoxy and condemned Arius' teaching that Christ was the first creation of God. The creed adopted by the council described Christ as, "God of God, Light of Light, very God of very God, begotten, not made, being of one substance (*homoousios*) with the Father."

Nicea did not end the controversy, however. Debate over how the creed (especially the phrase "one substance") ought to be interpreted continued to rage for decades. One group advocated the doctrine that Christ was a "similar substance" (*homoiousios*) as the Father. But for the most part, the issue of the Trinity was settled at Nicea and, by the fifth century, never again became a focus of serious controversy."

SOURCE: http://www.religionfacts.com/christianity/beliefs/trinity.htm 04/16/09

We learned from the prior history that bishop Athanasius led the opposition to Arius' teachings at the council of Nicea. We also learned that extra-biblical writers as early as the end of the first century gave hints of Trinitarian beliefs. Even Ignatius had writings dating circa **AD 100** exclaiming, "God himself appearing in the form of a man for the renewal of eternal life." While Tertullian seems to be the first who wrote about the trinity concept, his writings do not fully show the trinity concept adopted in the *Nicene Creed*. The *Athanasian Creed* surfaced and the version shown below is from the **1913** *Catholic Encyclopedia*. Some scholars believe that the *Athanasian Creed* appeared prior to the Council of Nicea in **AD 325**. Others believe it appeared in the fifth century and was not actually written by bishop Athanasius. I offer it here for discussion and so that the Church trinity theology can be more fully explored. Statements in this creed are discussed below.

The Athanasian Creed
Helps us understand Catholic Trinity theology!

"Whosoever will be saved, before all things it is necessary that he hold the Catholic Faith. Which Faith except everyone do keep whole and undefiled, without doubt he shall perish everlastingly. And the Catholic Faith is this, that we worship one God in Trinity and Trinity in Unity. Neither confounding the Persons, nor dividing the Substance. For there is one Person of the Father, another of the Son, and another of the Holy Ghost. But the Godhead of the Father, of the Son and of the Holy Ghost is all One, the Glory Equal, the Majesty Co-Eternal. Such as the Father is, such is the Son, and such is the Holy Ghost. The Father Uncreated, the Son Uncreated, and the Holy Ghost Uncreated. The Father Incomprehensible, the Son Incomprehensible, and the Holy Ghost Incomprehensible. The Father Eternal, the Son Eternal, and the Holy Ghost Eternal and yet they are not Three Eternals but One Eternal. As also there are not Three Uncreated, nor Three Incomprehensibles, but One Uncreated, and One Incomprehensible. So likewise the Father is Almighty, the Son Almighty, and the Holy Ghost Almighty. And yet they are not Three Almightiest but One Almighty.

So the Father is God, the Son is God, and the Holy Ghost is God. And yet they are not Three Gods, but One God. So likewise the Father is Lord, the Son Lord, and the Holy Ghost Lord. And yet not Three Lords but One Lord. For, like as we are compelled by the Christian verity to acknowledge every Person by Himself to be God and Lord, so are we forbidden by the Catholic Religion to say, there be Three Gods or Three Lords. The Father is made of none, neither created, nor begotten. The Son is of the Father alone; not made, nor created, but begotten. The Holy Ghost is of the Father, and of the Son neither made, nor created, nor begotten, but proceeding.

So there is One Father, not Three Fathers; one Son, not Three Sons; One Holy Ghost, not Three Holy Ghosts. And in this Trinity none is afore or after Other, None is greater or less than Another, but the whole Three Persons are Co-eternal together, and Co-equal. So that in all things, as is aforesaid, the Unity is Trinity, and the Trinity is Unity is to be worshipped. He therefore that will be saved, must thus think of the Trinity.

Furthermore, it is necessary to everlasting Salvation, that he also believe rightly the Incarnation of our Lord Jesus Christ. For the right Faith is, that we believe and confess, that our Lord Jesus Christ, the Son of God, is God and Man.

God, of the substance of the Father, begotten before the worlds; and Man, of the substance of His mother, born into the world. Perfect God and Perfect Man, of a reasonable Soul and human Flesh subsisting. Equal to the Father as touching His Godhead, and inferior to the Father as touching His Manhood. Who, although He be God and Man, yet He is not two, but One Christ. One, not by conversion of the Godhead into Flesh, but by taking of the Manhood into God. One altogether, not by confusion of substance, but by Unity of Person. For as the reasonable soul and flesh is one Man, so God and Man is one Christ. Who suffered for our salvation, descended into Hell, rose again the third day from the dead. He ascended into Heaven, He sitteth on the right hand of the Father, God Almighty, from whence he shall come to judge the quick and the dead. At whose coming all men shall rise again with their bodies, and shall give account for their own works. And they that have done good shall go into life everlasting, and they that have done evil into everlasting fire. This is the Catholic Faith, which except a man believe faithfully and firmly, he cannot be saved."

SOURCE: Catholic 1913 Athanasian Creed as found in Wikisource at the following URL http://en.wikisource.org/wiki/Catholic_Enclycopedia_(1913)/The_Athanasian_Creed.

Athanasian Creed Exegesis

Under the guise of "ordinary" humans not being able to fully comprehend God, the *Nicene Creed* was rationalized at the Council of Nicea **AD 325**. Ergo, the "trinity" is a "mystery" nobody will fully understand. The above *Athanasian Creed* is in essence the *Nicene Creed* with more detail than the current *Catholic Profession of Faith Creed*, which is also examined. In the creed exegesis that follows, I will contrast Scriptures with trinity dogma statements. There are many obviously idiotic statements in the *Athanasian Creed*. Perhaps that is why it is not the one currently used by the Church. Maybe it is too much detail? Yet, the statements within this creed are exactly what the Church uses as the basis of its trinity doctrine. Ergo, the *Athanasian Creed* fully explains the Church trinity doctrine, while some other creeds somewhat obscure the full Church doctrine.

Dogma Statement #1: No trinity belief, no salvation

"Whosoever will be saved, before all things it is necessary that he hold the Catholic Faith. Which Faith except everyone do keep whole and undefiled, without doubt he shall perish everlastingly. And the Catholic Faith is this, that we worship one God in Trinity and Trinity in Unity."

Translation: If you don't believe in the trinity doctrine and all other doctrines of the Catholic Faith, you are destined to perish in Hell. Even in 2009, this fear is in the minds of many Catholics who have been raised for centuries believing anyone outside of this faith will perish and is not saved. No trinity belief, no salvation is the teaching!

Scripture Refutation: The following twenty-five Scripture teachings directly challenge the salvation teaching found in the trinity creed. Nowhere in Scripture will you find the idea that if you don't believe in the trinity that you are not saved. In contrast, the Bible teaches about "repentance and righteousness" as being keys to our salvation. Ergo, obeying the Ten Commandments mean salvation! Yet, what about the deleted second commandment of the Catholic Church and its practice of "images and bowing down?" In any case, it is clear that belief in the trinity doctrine does not factor into God's salvation teachings found in Scripture. Yet, just the opposite is evidenced. Remember, John 3:36 where the wrath of God is still upon those who do not obey Jesus? Well then, what about Jesus' teaching about his God being the FATHER in John 20:17? Do you believe Jesus?

Twenty-Five Salvation Truths

#	Salvation Teaching from God's Word	Says Who	Reference
1	Salvation belongs to Yahweh	David	Psalms 3:8
2	Salvation belongs to Yahweh	John	Rev. 7:10
3	Salvation belongs also to the Lamb (Jesus)	John	Rev. 7:10
4	Salvation belongs to Yahweh	Jesus	John 5:26
5	Salvation belongs also to the Son (Jesus)	Jesus	John 5:26
6	Whoever praises Yahweh has salvation	Yahweh	Psalms 50:23
7	Whoever orders his conduct aright has salvation	Yahweh	Psalms 50:23
8	Whoever believes in Yahweh has salvation	Jesus	John 5:24
9	Whoever calls on name of Yahweh has salvation	Yahweh	Joel 2:32
10	Whoever believes unto righteousness has salvation	Paul	Romans 10:10
11	Whoever obeys what Jesus taught has salvation	Jesus	Luke 6:46
12	Whoever is awake to righteousness has salvation	Paul	1 Cor. 15:34
13	Whoever does not sin has salvation	Paul	Romans 4:8
14	Whoever is set free from sin has salvation	Paul	Romans 6:22
15	Whoever believes in Yahweh via Christ has salvation	John	John 3:16
16	Whoever is faithful to the LORD God has salvation	Yahweh	Ezekiel 18:9
17	Whoever turns away from wickedness has salvation	Yahweh	Ezekiel 18:21
18	Whoever gets a new heart and spirit has salvation	Yahweh	Ezekiel 18:31
19	Benefactors of righteous prayers may have salvation	Yahweh	Ezekiel 14:14
20	Benefactors of apostle's forgiveness have salvation	Jesus	John 20:20
21	Obeying the Ten Commandments means salvation	Jesus	Matt 19:17
22	Having a minimum righteousness means salvation	Jesus	Matt 5:20
23	Obeying two great commandments means salvation	Jesus	Matt 22:40
24	Righteous people will see salvation	Solomon	Wisdom 5:2
25	Righteous people will see salvation	Jesus	Matt 13:43

Dogma Statement #2: Equal Glory

"But the Godhead of the Father, of the Son and of the Holy Ghost is all One, the Glory Equal, the Majesty Co-Eternal."

> **Jesus said: "Whoever is ashamed of me and of my words in this faithless and sinful generation, the Son of Man will be ashamed of when he comes in his FATHER'S glory with the holy angels." Mark 8:38 (NAB)**
>
> **Jesus said: "I come in the FATHER'S glory!"**
>
> **Jesus said: "Just as the living FATHER sent me and I have life because of the FATHER, so also the one who feeds on me will have life because of me." John 6:57 (NAB)**
>
> **Jesus said: "I live because of the FATHER!"**

Scripture Facts: Jesus comes in his FATHER'S glory, not his own! Jesus lives because of the FATHER and not of his own accord. Which words are easiest for you to understand? Doesn't Jesus' statements make more sense to you? Who will you believe? The Catholic Church or Jesus? Note that the above verses are from the Catholic *New American Bible*.

Dogma Statement #3: Three Eternals, But One Eternal

"The Father Eternal, the Son Eternal, and the Holy Ghost Eternal and yet they are not Three Eternals but One Eternal."

> **Jesus said: "And to the angel of the church of Laodicea, write: These things saith the Amen, the faithful and true witness, <u>who</u> is the beginning of the creation of God." Revelation 3:14 (Douay-Rheims)**
>
> **Paul said: "He [Jesus] is the image of the invisible God, the firstborn of all creation." Colossians 1:15 (NAB)**
>
> **"The LORD [God] begot me [Jesus], the first-born of HIS ways, the forerunner of HIS prodigies of long ago; from of old I was poured forth, at the first, before the earth. When there were no depths I was brought forth, when there were no fountains or springs of water; before the mountains were settled into place, before the hills, I was brought forth; while as yet the earth and the fields were not made, nor the first clods of the world. When HE established the heavens I was there, when HE marked out the vault over the face of the deep; when HE made firm the skies above, when HE fixed fast the foundations of the earth; when he set for the sea its limit, so that the waters should not transgress his command; then was I beside HIM as HIS craftsman, and I was HIS delight day by day, playing before HIM all the while, playing on the surface of HIS earth; and I found delight in the sons of men." Proverbs 8:22-31 (NAB)**

Scripture Facts: Jesus was the first thing that God created in Douay-Rheims. Jesus was then used in the rest of God's creation as a craftsman working for God. But, Rev 3:14 in the NAB reads: "Jesus is the source of God's creation." This is a trinity doctrine-based translation, which doesn't reveal the truth. It obscures Jesus being created first by God, yet the NAB teaches this in Colossians 1:15 and Proverbs 8:22-31. And, it is God's creation, not Jesus'. Ergo, Jesus cannot be *the* "source" of God's creation. It is HIS!

Idiotic Statement: Dogma statement #3 in the creed reads like something that would come out of the mouth of a modern day politician. Think about it. We are TOLD, "There is Eternal 1, Eternal 2, and Eternal 3. Yet not three Eternals, but 1." It's psychobabble that now has relatively intelligent people acting like idiots! Didn't God give us a strong mind? Is not, in fact, the very mind of God HIMSELF dwelling in all true believers? Well, what's up? Who do you know that mouths psychobabble like this? Lawyers and politicians! Yes, and that must be who crafted the trinity doctrine at Nicea in **AD 325**. It certainly wasn't men of God, as Scripture does not back up the dogmatic trinity assertions in the creed.

Dogma Statement #4: Three Gods, But One God

"So the Father is God, the Son is God, and the Holy Ghost is God. And yet they are not Three Gods, but One God."

> **Jesus said: "Stop holding on to me, for I have not yet ascended to the FATHER. But go to my brothers and tell them, 'I am going to my FATHER and your FATHER, to my God and your God.' " John 20:17 (NAB)**
>
> **Jesus taught: "The FATHER is our God!"**

Scripture Facts: Jesus taught in clear and unambiguous language who our God is.

Idiotic Statement: Dogma statement #4 in the creed also reads like something that would come out of the mouth of a lawyer or politician. We are TOLD, "There is God 1, God 2, and God 3. Yet not three Gods, but 1." It's also psychobabble for those who are ignorant of Scripture: To program a belief in the trinity under the threat of no eternal life.

Dogma Statement #5: Three Lords, But One Lord

"So likewise the Father is Lord, the Son Lord, and the Holy Ghost Lord. And yet not Three Lords but One Lord."

> **Paul said: "Yet for us there is one God, the FATHER, from whom all things are and for whom we exist, and one Lord, Jesus Christ, through whom all things are and through whom we exist."**
> **1 Corinthian 8:6 (NAB)**
>
> **Paul taught: "There is only one Lord, Jesus Christ!"**

Scripture Facts: Paul makes it clear that there is only one Lord or master, Jesus Christ.

Idiotic Statement: Dogma statement #5 in the creed is also idiotic. We are TOLD, "There is Lord 1, Lord 2, and Lord 3. Yet not three Lords, but 1." It's also psychobabble used to "program" those without knowledge of these key Scriptures. Do you believe what was obviously written by skilled lawyers and politicians who word-smithed the trinity creed statement or do you believe Jesus and Paul in their opposing Scripture statements? Who is the liar about the trinity? Jesus and Paul? Scripture? The Church?

Dogma Statement #6: Forbidden to say three Gods, three Lords

"We are compelled by the Christian verity to acknowledge every Person by Himself to be God and Lord, so are we forbidden by the Catholic Religion to say, there be Three Gods or Three Lords."

Idiotic Statement: Dogma statement #6 in the creed asks you to publicly state that the Father, the Son and the Holy Spirit are all God and all Lord, but then, after stating three Gods and three Lords, you must never say there are three Gods and three Lords. This goes well beyond idiocy and straight into cult programming. What about the fact that people were killed because they would not agree to make such idiotic proclamations?

Dogma Statement #7: None is greater; they are all equal

"And in this Trinity none is afore or after Other, None is greater or less than Another, but the whole Three Persons are Co-eternal together, and Co-equal."

> **Jesus said: "You heard me tell you, 'I am going away and I will come back to you.' If you loved me, you would rejoice that I am going to the FATHER; for the FATHER is greater than I." John 14:28 (NAB)**
>
> **Paul said: "Have among yourselves the same attitude that is also yours in Christ Jesus, who, though he was in the form of God, did not regard equality with God something to be grasped."**
> **Philippians 3:5-6 (NAB)**

Scripture Facts: Dogma statement #7 in the creed asks you to believe in the equality of all three persons in the trinity god. Yet, Jesus makes it clear that he is not equal to God [FATHER] whom he taught was "greater!" Then, we have Paul's teaching that Jesus never regarded equality with God as something "to be grasped." Yes, it's in the Catholic Bible!

A Pattern Of Deception Emerges

I am going to stop at number 7. I could go on and even deeper into the exegesis of this trinity creed, but there is no point. This creed has one obvious pattern that emerges. It is a pattern of deliberately ignoring the teachings found in Scripture. The creed ignores God's Word, but especially the teachings of Jesus and of Paul. Who will you believe? Are you going to believe a creed that appears as psychobabble from lawyers or politicians? Well, men of God did not create the trinity doctrine! Men of God would not pervert HIS Word in such deceptive ways. Will you believe the trinity creed or Jesus? Paul? God HIMSELF?

The Deceivers & The Deceived

Paul said: "In fact, all who want to live religiously in Christ Jesus will be persecuted. But wicked people and charlatans will go from bad to worse, deceivers and deceived. But you remain faithful to what you have learned and believed, because you know from whom you learned it, and that from infancy you have known (the) sacred scriptures, which are capable of giving you wisdom for salvation through faith in Christ Jesus." 2 Timothy 3:12-15 (NAB)

Paul taught that wicked people and "charlatans" go from bad to worse deceiving other people and themselves being deceived. This is what exactly is happening with the trinity doctrine. Those who should know better are deceived and in turn deceive others. What keeps you in truth and gives you wisdom? Paul gives the answer saying, "from infancy you have known the sacred Scriptures, which are capable of giving you wisdom for salvation through faith in Christ Jesus." It's not a deceptive doctrine; it is Scripture!

The Church As Pillar Of Truth

Paul said: "But if I should be delayed, you should know how to behave in the household of God, which is the church of the living God, the pillar and foundation of truth." 1 Timothy 3:15 (NAB)

What Apostle Paul is teaching us here is that the Church is supposed to be the "pillar" and "foundation" of truth. This means the Church was supposed to be a strong supporter of God's truth. It does not mean that the Church itself <u>defines</u> truth! You've already learned that it is God's Word that is truth, all of it. You also learned in the first three lessons from Jesus and God that the Church would lie to you! Even negate God's Word!

"Sanctify them in truth. THY word is truth." John 17:17 (Douay-Rheims)

"YOUR every word is enduring; all YOUR just edicts are forever."
                                                        Psalms 199:160 (NAB)

Most churches and especially the Catholic Church profess to hold Scripture as close to their hearts as they hold the Eucharist. That's close! However, how can we say that the Church is a "pillar" of God's truth when it has ignored Scripture and has created the trinity doctrine? Woe to all who teach that the Church can negate a single word in God's Holy Bible. Or, who would say that the Church itself *is* truth! Woe indeed. And, if the Church lies about the very nature of God and of HIS human Son, what does that mean for the salvation of the people who attend the Church? Are they saved? Are they engaged in idolatry? This much I know for sure. The Church negates God's commandments and it lies about the nature of God. The effects of such errors will lead many to Hell. LORD, have mercy on the many deceived Christians in the world.

LORD, open the eyes of YOUR people to Holy Scripture!

Trinity Dogma © 2009 Rev. Edward G. Palmer

Catholic Basis Of Trinity Doctrine

What Scripture does the Catholic Church use to rationalize its trinity doctrine, if any? There must be some Scripture. Yes, there is, and it is summarized as follows:

"The datum for Christian theology is first of all Christ himself. On the one hand, he called God his Father, prayed to him, loved him, taught his teaching, and obeyed his will. On the other hand, he claimed to be one with, and equal to, the Father. And he also promised to send the Spirit. The scriptural data from which the Church derives the doctrine of the Trinity are essentially

    a. That there is only one God (Deut 6:4);
    b. That the Father is God (Jn 5:18);
    c. That the Son is God (Jn 8:58); and
    d. That the Holy Spirit is God (Mt 28:19)

The data are historical: God's progressive revelation of himself, first as the transcendent Creator 'outside' us; then as the incarnate Savior 'beside' us; then as the indwelling Spirit 'inside' us. The reason for this progression, first Father (Old Testament), then Son (Gospels), then Spirit (Acts of the Apostles and the Church), is found in God's very being, which is love (1 Jn 4:18), and in the purpose and motive for God's self-revelation to man, which is love. For love's aim is always greater intimacy, deeper union with the beloved; so the stages of God's self-revelation are stages of increasing intimacy with man (from 'outside' to 'beside' to 'inside')."

SOURCE: Kreeft, Peter J. (2001) *Catholic Christianity, A Complete Catechism of Catholic Beliefs based on the Catechism of the Catholic Church*, p40, Ignatius Press, San Francisco.

New American Bible Scriptures

"Hear, O Israel! The LORD is our God, the LORD alone!" Deut 6:4

"For this reason the Jews tried all the more to kill him, because he not only broke the Sabbath but he also called God his own FATHER, making himself equal to God." John 5:18

Jesus said to them, "Amen, amen, I say to you, before Abraham came to be, I am." John 8:58

"Go, therefore, and make disciples of all nations, baptizing them in the name of the FATHER, and of the Son, and of the Holy Spirit."
                                              Matthew 28:19

Commentary On Trinity Basis

Peter J. Kreeft, Ph.D., is a Professor of Philosophy at Boston College and the best-selling author of over 25 books. His book *Catholic Christianity* is recognized as providing the "essential elements of Catholic Christianity." Having taken this description from the book, I find the description of the trinity basis above similar in nature to the *Athanasian Creed* and absolutely Catholic in nature. Kreeft talks about the evolving of God's love through progressive revelations. God reveals HIMSELF first as the Father, then as the Son and at last, as the Holy Spirit. Ergo, God manifests HIMSELF in three distinct persons. Is this the same God who taught us in Malachi that HE doesn't change? And did not Jesus change from Spirit (descending) to Man (ascending) to Spirit?

> **"Surely I, the LORD, do not change!" Malachi 3:6 (NAB)**

Is this the same God Jesus taught in John 20:17?

> **Jesus said: "But go to my brothers and tell them, 'I am going to my FATHER and your FATHER, to my God and your God.' " John 20:17 (NAB)**

Is this the same God that Paul taught us about in 1 Corinthians 8:6?

> **Paul said: "Yet for us there is one God, the FATHER!" 1 Cor 8:6 (NAB)**

Is this the same God that is not a man or human?

> **"<u>God is not man</u> that HE should speak falsely, <u>nor human</u>, that HE should change his mind. Is HE one to speak and not act, to decree and not fulfill?" Numbers 23:19 (NAB)**

The progressive revelation of God's love makes for good trinity rationalization and Church theology, but it does not excuse the willful refusal to acknowledge whom Jesus and Paul taught was God. Nor can it excuse the willful refusal to acknowledge those attributes of God that are revealed within Scripture such as Numbers 23:19. Christians should be worshipping the God of the Jews. That is exactly who Jesus and Paul and all the other apostles worshipped. Instead, the false trinity doctrine has been created. Just because the Jews thought Jesus was God when he said, "I am" — does not mean he meant it that way. To believe this error makes Jesus a liar throughout many of his other teachings. Indeed, everyone who is with God is one with HIM. That is the teaching of our Lord Jesus. Jesus also did not just call God his FATHER! Jesus also called God our FATHER! And, how does baptizing people in the name of the FATHER, the Son and the Holy Spirit make the Holy Spirit God? And what about Peter's teaching to baptize in the name of Jesus? Do we baptize in the name of the Holy Spirit to receive the Holy Spirit?

> **"[Peter] ordered them to be baptized in the name of Jesus Christ."**
> **Acts 10:48 (NAB)**

Peter said: "I remembered the word of the Lord [Jesus], how he had said, 'John baptized with water but you will be baptized with the Holy Spirit.' " Acts 11:16 (NAB)

The answer to the last question is no, we don't. We baptize people in the name of Jesus Christ. That is what the Spirit has just imparted to me. Becoming baptized in the name of Jesus results in receiving the Holy Spirit. Ergo, Matthew 28:19 appears to be a "tinkered" verse designed to support the trinity doctrine. Don't cherry pick Scripture; believe all of God's Word. How does Matthew 28:19 make "God the Holy Spirit?" There is only one way and that is by using the trinity doctrine to interpret Scripture. How does John 5:18 make Jesus God when Jesus specifically taught us that he wasn't God? Again, Scripture is being interpreted through the trinity doctrine. Don't do it. Allow God's Word to speak for itself. I've already discussed this earlier. The Church has no justification in Scripture for its trinity doctrine. It was at the beginning a man-made doctrine conjured up for political and religious reasons in Constantine's Roman Empire. There was no divinely inspired moment, because God does not inspire teachings that speak against Scripture.

Trinity Doctrine Is Baseless In Scripture!

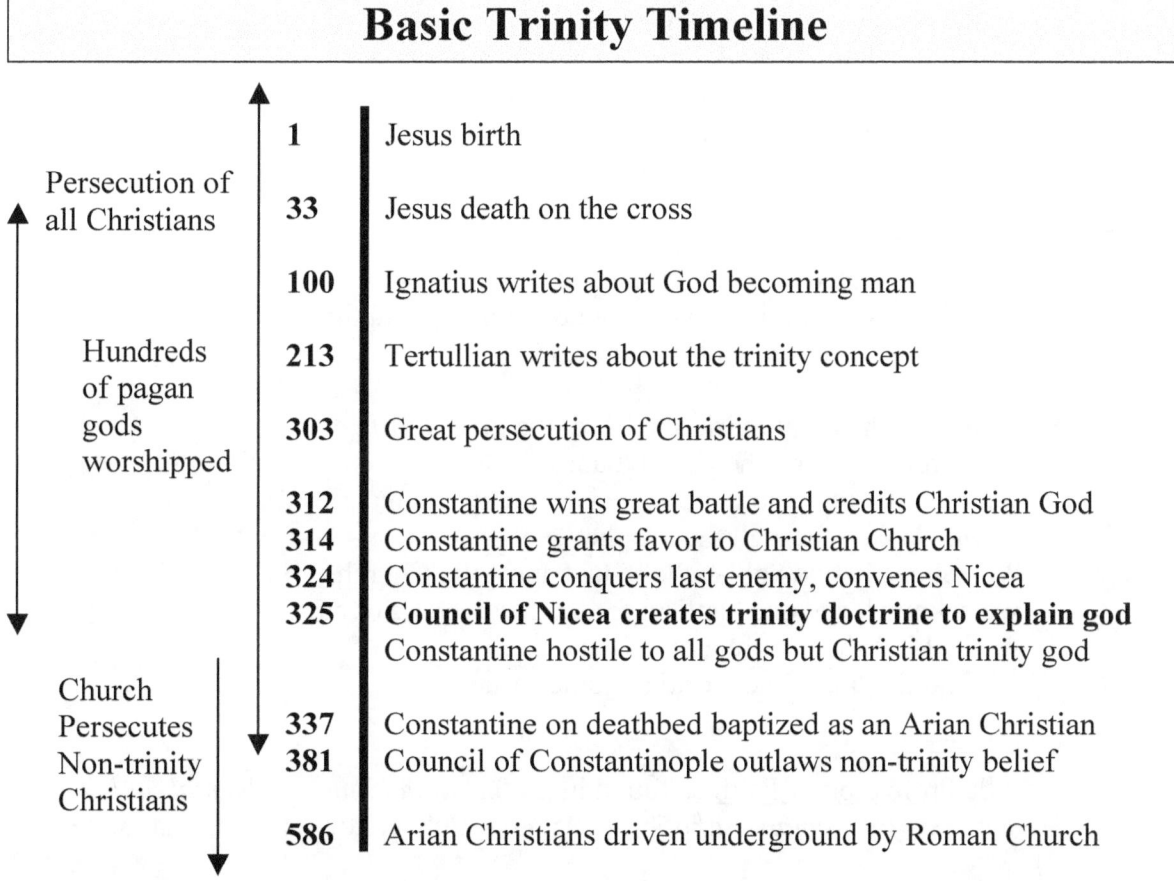

The Church created its trinity doctrine at the direction of emperor Constantine in the context of hundreds of pagan gods, political strife and religious division in Christianity.

Trinity Dogma © 2009 Rev. Edward G. Palmer

The Catholic <u>Profession Of Faith</u> in 2009

We believe in one God,
    The FATHER, the Almighty,
    Maker of Heaven and earth,
    Of all that is seen and unseen.

We believe in one Lord, Jesus Christ,
    The only Son of God,
    Eternally begotten of the FATHER,
    God from God, Light from Light,
    True God from true God,
    Begotten, not made, one in Being with the FATHER.
    Through him all things were made.
    For us men and for our salvation he came down from Heaven:

All bow at the following words up to: and became man.

By the power of the Holy Spirit
    He was born of the Virgin Mary, <u>and became man</u>.
For our sake he was crucified under Pontius Pilate;
    He suffered, died, and was buried.
    On the third day he rose again
    In fulfillment of the Scriptures:
    He ascended into Heaven
    And is seated at the right hand of the FATHER.
He will come again in glory to judge the living and the dead,
    And his kingdom will have no end.

We believe in the Holy Spirit, the Lord, the giver of life,
    Who proceeds from the FATHER and the Son.
    With the FATHER and the Son he is worshipped and glorified.
    He has spoken through the Prophets.
    We believe in one holy catholic and apostolic Church.
    We acknowledge one baptism for the forgiveness of sins.
    We look for the resurrection of the dead,
        And the life of the world to come. Amen.

Catholic <u>Profession of Faith</u> as found in (2002) *RitualSong, A Hymnal and Service Book for Roman Catholics,* p295, GIA Publications, Inc., Chicago.

The *Catholic Profession of Faith* shown above is essentially the *Nicene Creed*, which resulted from the first two ecumenical Councils (in AD 325 and AD 381).

Scripture Errors In 2009 Catholic Profession Of Faith

Scripture Truth

> We believe in one God,
>   The FATHER, the Almighty,
>   Maker of Heaven and earth,
>   Of all that is seen and unseen.
> We believe in one Lord, Jesus Christ,

There are "Sons of God" - Mt 5:9; Lk 20:36; Rom 8:14, 19; Gal 3:26. Ergo, this should read "the only begotten Son." Mt 12:49-50

"First Created" Rev 3:14; Col 1:15; Proverbs 8:22-30. Ergo, Jesus was created, not eternal.

Jesus was "Made just like us" Hebrews 2:17
"God is FATHER" John 20:17; 1 Cor 8:6;
"Unequal" Phil 2:5-6; 1 Tim 2:5; Rev 1:1

>   The only Son of God,
>   Eternally begotten of the FATHER,
>   God from God, Light from Light,
>   True God from true God,
>   Begotten, not made, one in Being with the FATHER.

Scripture Truth

> Through him all things were made.
> For us men and for our salvation he came down from Heaven:

~~All bow at the following words up to: and became man.~~

Scripture Truth Note: Jesus was born a human like all humans are born. It's God's kingdom and God returns after Jesus does. Rev 21:3-8

> By the power of the Holy Spirit
>   He was born of the Virgin Mary~~, and became man~~.
> For our sake he was crucified under Pontius Pilate;
>   He suffered, died, and was buried.
>   On the third day he rose again
>   In fulfillment of the Scriptures:
>   He ascended into Heaven
>   And is seated at the right hand of the FATHER.
> He will come again in glory to judge the living and the dead,
>   And ~~his~~ [God's] kingdom will have no end.

1 John 1:3 Fellowship is with "God and Son".

Matthew 4:10 Worship only God who Jesus and Paul taught is the FATHER. Revelation 22:9

Jesus taught that John's Baptism also resulted in salvation [Mt 21:31-32]. There is only one Spirit baptism into one body [1 Cor 12:13]. Also, See Eph 4:1-6, Acts 1:4, Acts 8:37, Acts 10:47-48, Acts 19:5, Acts 22:15-16, & Rom 6:4.

> We believe in the Holy Spirit, the Lord, the giver of life,
>   Who proceeds from the FATHER and the Son.
>   With the FATHER and the Son he is worshipped and glorified.
>   He has spoken through the Prophets.

Hebrews 1:1 "God spoke" through the Prophets.

John 15:26 "Spirit proceeds from the FATHER."

> We believe in one holy catholic and apostolic Church.
> We acknowledge [there is only] one [Spirit] baptism
>   [Into one body] for the forgiveness of sins. [1 Cor 12:13]
> We look for the resurrection of the dead,
>   And the life of the world to come. Amen.

Notes
1. Scripture supports white-boxed areas except as noted by grayed lines.
2. Grey creed areas are not supported by Scripture, but only by Church dogma.
3. Church *was* supposed to be the pillar and foundation of God's truth [1 Tim 3:15].

Trinity Dogma © 2009 Rev. Edward G. Palmer

Work Out Your Salvation

I've listened many times to the priest pray: "God, look upon the faith of your Church and not the sins of the people." Looking at the Catholic *Profession of Faith*, I can understand why. Yet, God in HIS new covenant with man does not look upon groups of people or the Church collectively. God holds each man, woman and child accountable for their own sins. Ergo, the priest's prayer is worthless and indicates a lack of fully understanding God's salvation. With all the idolatry built into the Christian creeds and worship services, and not just Catholic but all Trinitarian churches, is it any wonder that the Apostle Paul taught us to work out with fear and trembling our salvation?

> **Paul said: "So then, my beloved, obedient as you have always been, not only when I am present but all the more now when I am absent, work out your salvation with fear and trembling." Phil. 2:12 (NAB)**

You Are Misled And Like Angels

> **Jesus said to them in reply, "You are misled because you do not know the scriptures or the power of God. At the resurrection they neither marry nor are given in marriage but are like the angels in Heaven."**
> **Matthew 22:29-30 (NAB)**

If you understand that Jesus was made exactly like us so he could be a faithful high priest before God for us, and if you understand he was the firstborn again in the resurrection, and if you understand we will be like him — then maybe you can understand we will be like angels in the resurrection? Just like Jesus is now. Maybe then it will make sense to you when Paul writes about him "coming back with the voice of an archangel?"

Get Your Praise From God

> **Paul said: "One is not a Jew outwardly. True circumcision is not outward, in the flesh. Rather, one is a Jew inwardly, and circumcision is of the heart, in the spirit, not the letter; his praise is not from human beings but from God." Romans 2:28-29 (NAB)**

In case you're wondering about how to worship God, you need to realize HE is inside of you in Spirit and in the heavens above. Therefore, don't look to any physical object on this earth to direct your worship towards. Look inside and towards the heavens and give all the Glory to the invisible God of our Lord Jesus Christ. HE is the "living God" the Bible talks about. When you worship God, worship HIM just like Jesus did. And, if you are truly saved, your heart will have been transformed and your soul will have been returned to the God that Jesus worshipped and served. In such a case, you will not get your "praise from human beings, but from God."

Give the invisible God YAHWEH your worship. That's what Jesus did!

Trinity Dogma © 2009 Rev. Edward G. Palmer

Is Your Brain Wired for Social Conformity?

If you've read the "*The Message*," you are already aware of the reticular activating system (RAS) and the role it plays when it comes to determining what your brain will accept or reject as important information. Go back and read *The Message* if you don't recall the RAS completely. In short, your own beliefs may stand in your way of being able to perceive God's truth. Ergo, you continue to believe the trinity, because you've always been taught the trinity and the RAS automatically rejects conflicting information. It's the old adage of "repeat a lie long enough and it will take on the attribute of being the truth." This is exactly what the trinity doctrine is; it's a lie that has been repeated for over 1684 years. It is now dogmatic and Christians assume it to be the truth. However, it isn't just the "reticular activating system" you need to be concerned about in your search for truth. Your mind also works to "conform" your beliefs to the majority view. Are you wired for "social conformity?" A recent health study suggests that you are.

Brain May Be Wired for Social Conformity
Study says 'error-monitoring' signals keep us from being too different from others

(HealthDay News) -- Your brain may be wired to go along with popular opinion in social situations, a new study suggests.

Scans done with functional magnetic resonance imaging showed that people whose opinion differed with that of a group of people experienced a neuronal response in the brain's rostral cingulate zone (RCZ) and nucleus acumens (NAc) -- areas that seem to help monitor behavioral outcomes and anticipate and process rewards as well as social learning, respectively.

This signal appears to tell the brain a "prediction error" has occurred, which seems to cause an adjustment in the long-term to an individual's own opinion. The magnitude of the signal appears to correlate with differences in conforming behavior across subjects, the study said. The findings were published n the January 15, 2009 issue of *Neuron*.

"The present study explains why we often automatically adjust our opinion in line with the majority opinion," study author Vasily Klucharev, from the F.C. Donders Center for Cognitive Neuroimaging in the Netherlands, said in a news release issued by the journal's publisher. "Our results also show that social conformity is based on mechanisms that comply with reinforcement learning and is reinforced by the neural error-monitoring activity which signals what is probably the most fundamental social mistake — that of being too different from others." SOURCE: Cell Press, news release, Jan. 14, 2009

Vitacost Newsletter, Health Daily, February 9, 2009

You Need To Love Truth!

[Because they are not 'lovers of the truth'], "God is sending them a <u>deceiving power</u> so that they may believe the lie, that all who have not believed the truth but have approved wrong doing may be condemned." 2 Thessalonians 3:11-12 (NAB)

You Need To Renew Your Mind!

"Do not conform yourselves to this age but be transformed by the renewal of your mind, that you may discern what is the will of God, what is good and pleasing and perfect." Romans 12:2 (NAB)

So, we saw in "*The Message*" that at the base of our brain we have the RAS, the reticular activating system that filters what our brains will even consider. Now we learn that other parts of our brains may even "adjust our opinion" to conform to the majority opinion. Could it be that this is the "deceiving power" Paul talks about above? I do believe the trinity is the "great deception" talked about in Scripture. However, this much I know is absolute truth, straight from God's Holy Word. God can change our opinions!

When you sincerely receive within your heart, our Lord Jesus Christ as God's sole and only human sacrifice for your lost soul, God will send HIS Spirit of Truth to dwell within you and HE will guide you with HIS Spirit into all truth. Thus, a sincere acceptance of our Lord Jesus Christ leads to a renewing of our mind so that we can recognize God's Word. You've already learned that truth is defined by what is contained in Scripture. That truth is HIS Word unaltered by scribes seeking to support Church doctrine.

> **"But when [Jesus], the kindness and generous love of God our savior appeared, not because of any righteous deeds we had done but because of HIS mercy, HE saved us through the bath of rebirth and renewal by the Holy Spirit, whom HE richly poured out on us through Jesus Christ our savior, so that we might be justified by HIS grace and become heirs in hope of eternal life." Titus 3:4-7 (NAB)**
>
> **[The Holy Spirit] "HE poured out on us abundantly through Jesus Christ our Savior." Titus 3:6 (NKJV)**

The Holy Spirit Renews Your Mind!

So, we see "built-within" our bodies the desire to conform to majority opinion and not stick our necks out with a contrasting opinion. Don't think for a moment I have not felt the "social pressures" to conform to the "trinity lie." I have. Yet, I cannot help myself, for God HIMSELF dwells within me and guides me in HIS truth. Having received God's Holy Spirit means you will have a hunger for God's Word that will out weigh the influences of Church doctrine. "So, if the Son has set you free, you are free indeed." John 8:36 — Free from what? Free from the majority opinions in this world. Free to consider God's truth.

Is This Why Only A Few Find The Way?

Indeed, since God has created us, the "built-within" body and mind obstacles to truth I have cited are directly from HIM. Yet, in HIS DIVINE wisdom, HE has provided an "eternal" solution in Christ Jesus for all sincere "lovers of the truth."

Long before I ever knew God as I now know HIM, I already knew that I loved the truth. I have always been a truth seeker even if it meant I would take an unpopular position. Yet very few people I have met really want to know the truth. How about you? And, if you claim salvation in Jesus Christ, have you learned to love the word of God that he taught you? Have you learned to place HIS Word above that of the Church and its doctrines?

What about all the Scripture that speaks directly against the trinity doctrine? Will you believe the Word or will you seek to change the Word using Church doctrine? The choice is yours to make. However, this I know is truth, if you seek to change, alter or otherwise dismiss the words of God that I have presented to you in this book, you do not have the Spirit of Truth dwelling within you and, without question, your soul is in jeopardy. Only those who are lovers of the truth will find the way home. This is the "few" that Jesus refers to when he said, "few will find the way."

> **"Enter through the narrow gate; for the gate is wide and the road broad that leads to destruction, and those who enter through it are many. How narrow the gate and constricted the road that leads to life. And those who find it are few." Matthew 7:13-14 (NAB)**

Note: I am now primarily providing Scriptures from the <u>New American Bible</u>, which is the current Bible of the Roman Catholic Church. It is used as the basis of all Catholic theology. However, all other bibles have verses that are similar in wording as the NAB, with few exceptions. This is for the benefit of Catholic and other readers whose eyes are seldom exposed, while at Church, to actual Scripture read directly from an actual Bible.

Very Few Christians Read The Bible

It is regularly reported that as few as 15% of all people who call themselves a Christian actually read the Bible. I suspect that when it comes to Catholics, Lutherans and other main line denominations, that this may be as low as 5% or less. How can anyone know the truth about God if they do not read HIS Word? And, is the lack of being motivated to read HIS Word yet another sign of those who have never sincerely accepted Christ?

Very few Christians now believe God's Word, but almost all Christians believe the trinity doctrine!

Jesus warns us of a <u>FEW</u> and <u>MANY</u> in Mt 7:13-14!

"Jesus laid no claim to equality with God!"

"Take to heart yourselves what you find in Christ Jesus. He was in the form [image] of God; yet <u>he laid no claim to equality with God</u>, but made himself nothing, assuming the role of a slave. Bearing the human likeness, sharing the human lot, he humbled himself, and was obedient, even to the point of death, death on a cross! Therefore God raised him to the heights and bestowed on him the name above all names, that at the name of Jesus every knee should bow -- in Heaven, on earth, and in the depths -- and every tongue acclaim, 'Jesus Christ is Lord' [master] to the glory of God the FATHER."
Philippians 2:5-12 (REB) Revised English Bible

"Jesus did not regard equality with God something to be grasped." <u>Catholic</u> New American <u>Bible</u>!

"Have among yourselves the same attitude that is also yours in Christ Jesus,
Who, though he was in the form [image] of God,
    <u>did not regard equality with God something
        to be grasped</u>.
   Rather, he emptied himself,
   taking the form of a slave,
   coming in human likeness;
   and found human in appearance,
   he humbled himself,
   becoming obedient to death,
      even death on a cross.
Because of this, God greatly exalted him
   and bestowed on him the name
   that is above every name,
   that at the name of Jesus
   every knee should bend,
   of those in Heaven and on earth and under
      the earth,
   and every tongue confess that
   Jesus Christ is Lord [master],
   to the glory of God the FATHER."   Philippians 2:5-12 (NAB)

All bibles in the table below agree that Jesus was made human, just like you and I. We see this in Hebrews 2:17 and Philippians 2:7. In Philippians 2:6 we also see that Jesus *did not regard equality with God as something to be grasped by any human.* For those who want to believe Jesus is God, verse 6 implies it in some noted translations. However, immediately after verse 6, those same translations then state Jesus was only a human like you and I. Ergo, verse 6 reflects theological error and confusion within some translations.

Trinity Dogma © 2009 Rev. Edward G. Palmer

Jesus was <u>made</u> a human just like you and I.
Jesus was not equal to God and neither are you and I.

"[Jesus], though he was in the form of God, did not regard equality with God [as] something to be grasped." Philippians 2:6 (NAB)

#	Thirty-One Translations	Jesus "Made" Like Us Heb. 2:17	Jesus Human "Like Us" Phil. 2:7	Jesus Not Equal To God Phil. 2:6
1	New King James Version	✔	✔	1
2	Douay-Rheims	✔	✔	1
3	King James Version	✔	✔	1
4	New American Bible	✔	✔	✔
5	American Standard Version	✔	✔	✔
6	Amplified Bible	✔	✔	✔
7	Bible In Basic English	✔	✔	2
8	Contemporary English Version	✔	✔	3
9	Darby's Translation	✔	✔	✔
10	English Standard Version	✔	✔	✔
11	Geneva Bible	✔	✔	1
12	God's Word	✔	✔	4
13	Holman Christian Standard Bible	✔	✔	4
14	International Children's Bible	✔	✔	4
15	Phillips NT Bible*	✔	✔	5
16	New American Standard Bible	✔	✔	✔
17	New American Standard Bible 1977	✔	✔	✔
18	New Century Version	✔	✔	✔
19	New English Translation (NET)	✔	✔	✔
20	New International Version	✔	✔	✔
21	New Jerusalem Bible	✔	✔	✔
22	New Living Translation	✔	✔	3
23	New Revised Standard Version	✔	✔	✔
24	Revised English Bible	✔	✔	✔
25	Revised Standard Version	✔	✔	✔
26	The Living Bible	✔	✔	5
27	The Message	✔	✔	5
28	Wesley New Testament*	✔	✔	1
29	Today's English Version	✔	✔	5
30	Young's Literal Translation	✔	✔	1
31	James Moffatt Translation	✔	✔	✔
	*Substitute for Jewish Tanach in first table.	100% Agreement	100% Agreement	48% Agreement

Trinity Dogma © 2009 Rev. Edward G. Palmer

Table Notes:
1. [Jesus] being in the form of God did not consider it robbery to be equal with God.
2. In the form of God, it did not seem that to take for oneself was to be like God.
3. Christ was truly God. But he did not try to remain equal with God.
4. In the form of God and equal with God, he did not take advantage of this equality.
5. Who had always been God by nature, did not cling to his prerogatives as God's equal.

In the above table, the checkmarks are bibles that are fairly uniform using the language of the Catholic *New American Bible* concerning "grasped." This was 15 of the 31 bibles or 48% in agreement with the Catholic NAB language. Of the remaining bibles, 6 of the 16 or 37.5% used the cryptic statement shown in note 1 above. Quite frankly, I have no idea of what is meant by "did not consider it robbery to be equal with God." This is especially true when the very next verse states how Jesus emptied himself into human form just like you and I. Note 2 is equally cryptic language. However, notes 3-5 are similar to the NAB statement. I separated them out, because of the slightly different verbiage and especially in Note 3, where it reads, "Christ was truly God." This is clearly a man-made statement.

No believer should take comfort in such strange wording, given the teachings of Jesus in John 20:17 and elsewhere. These notes for Philippians 2:6 reflect theological error and the confusion in these particular bibles. I have already pointed out similar verses before. The bibles noted above also all have 100% agreement with the other bibles concerning whom Jesus and Paul taught was our God. And they all agree Jesus was human!

The Trinitarian Church lies and it does not know God!

Throughout this book, you have seen the trinity doctrine compared to God's Word. Church lies include teaching "God from God" and "Jesus was not made" in creeds. Not to mention countless other lies about God's Word. The Trinitarian Church lies about the nature of God and of Jesus Christ. Our Lord Jesus spoke well about such liars, even in today's Church. This book is a warning from God to the Christian Church. Set your house in order and get right, for lo, the time is near and you *will* be held accountable for your lies and apostasy. Indeed, the Trinitarian Church serves up Satan's lies about the nature of God and His human begotten Son Jesus. Verily, the father of lies is behind the trinity.

> **Jesus said; "You belong to your father the devil and you willingly carry out your father's desires. He was a murderer from the beginning and does not stand in truth, because there is no truth in him. When he tells a lie, he speaks in character, because he is a liar and the father of lies." John 8:44 (NAB)**

> **Jesus said: "If I glorify myself, my glory is worth nothing; but it is my FATHER who glorifies me, of whom you say, 'HE is our God.' You do not know HIM, but I know HIM. And if I should say that I do not know HIM, I would be like you a liar. But I do know HIM and I keep HIS word." John 8:54 (NAB)**

> **"Whoever belongs to God hears the words of God; for this reason you do not listen, because you do not belong to God." John 8:47 (NAB)**

Edward, What If You Are Mistaken?

I can already hear someone's voice, after all this, asking the question. "But Edward, what if you are mistaken about the trinity doctrine? What's going to happen when you come face to face with God?" I only expect to hear God say, "well done Edward," because,

The following facts about my teachings would still be true!

1. I've taught you only about what is in God's Word. It is not my word, but HIS!
2. I've obeyed the teachings of the Lord Jesus Christ and have taught them to you.
3. I have loved Jesus because I have obeyed him and have taught you to obey him.
4. I've worshipped the FATHER whom the Lord Jesus Christ taught me to worship.
5. I've worshipped the FATHER in Spirit and in Truth [and not in the trinity lie].
6. I've prayed to whom the Lord Jesus Christ taught me to pray to, the FATHER.
7. I've practiced righteousness as the Lord Jesus Christ taught me to do.
8. I've written what God HIMSELF has guided me to write for your edification.
9. I will have been faithful to the God whom Jesus taught me to love.
10. I do not engage in idolatrous Jesus worship of a god called "God the Son."
11. I do not engage in idolatrous Spirit worship of a god called "God the Holy Spirit."
12. I do not worship or bow down to carved/graven images, carved idols or a crucifix.
13. I do not interpret Scripture through Church doctrine. I accept the simple language of God's Word, which is written at a six-grade level so all could understand. I have taught people to obey God, keep HIS commandments and to study HIS Word.
14. I have exposed Satan's doctrines that seek to steal the souls of God's people.
15. I have taught you to read and study your Bible. Satan tries to confuse you about the Bible by saying you can't understand it without the help of a priest to interpret. Without question, you can understand it and that is what will save your soul.

And, What If I am Right?

David, the brother of my friend Marian once said, "Now Marian, if Edward is right, then everyone in our family and everyone for hundreds of years have been wrong. How could that be?" The answer is easy, I follow Jesus' teachings; I do not follow Church teachings.

> **Jesus said, "Enter by the narrow gate; for wide is the gate and broad is the way that leads to destruction, and there are many who go in by it. Because narrow is the gate and difficult is the way which leads to life, and there are few who find it." Matthew 7:13-14 (NKJV)**

Few people are now entering God's narrow gate of life!

Trinity Dogma © 2009 Rev. Edward G. Palmer

Conclusion

You believe Jesus is God, because ever since 325 AD the Church has taught a trinity dogma. All of your ancestors since 325 AD were taught this doctrine. And all throughout your own life you have been taught this lie. It is not by mistake. The trinity dogma was designed by Satan to steal souls away from God by getting people that were supposed to belong to HIM engaged in idolatrous worship of a "substitute" god. That is exactly what Jesus Christ has become for many Christians. A god of forgiveness has been substituted for the righteous God that Jesus himself served and worshipped. You will not find one iota of direct support for the trinity dogma within the Holy Bible. This man-made Church doctrine directly contradicts the simple and easy to understand teachings of Jesus Christ and Apostle Paul about God's identity. They both identified God as being the FATHER!

You *will* find a handful of verses in the Bible that have been altered by man to support the trinity dogma. That is why it is important to study with at least three different versions of Scripture as I pointed out earlier in this book. Yet, even when it comes to these "so-called" Scriptures, you are left with a basic choice. Will you believe what Jesus taught? Or, will you take on faith the words of your church that directly contradict the teachings of Jesus, especially when supported by man altered and errant verses?

Many years ago, while studying the Word in the pew of a church, God said: "It's time for you to choose, Edward. It's either the pastor's word or MINE!" My answer to God was directly from my heart. "It's YOUR Word FATHER!"

Now, you are here reading these words. God has asked me to pose the same question to you. Will you accept the simple words of our Lord Jesus Christ, whom God sent to us incarnate in human form as a man and whose purpose was to help bring us home? Or, is it more important to you to fully accept the doctrine of your church? For many, it will be the church they attend, because social pressures will override God's Word. However, you should choose wisely as your eternal soul is what is really at stake. If you choose the doctrine of your church over God's Word, you might as well set your Bible aside. The wisdom God has given us to live this life wisely is in the Bible and it will be of no further use to you if you do not give it priority and hold it supreme over church doctrines.

The message God told me to tell Christians is that many of them are headed towards Hell instead of Heaven, as they currently believe. The entire message God gave me is contained in the *Book of Edward: Christian Mythology*. Jesus teaches us that he will reject many who call him "Lord, Lord." Are you one of those whom Jesus will reject?

> **Jesus said, "Not everyone who says to me, 'Lord, Lord,' shall enter the kingdom of Heaven, but he who does the will of my FATHER in Heaven. Many will say to me in that day, 'Lord, Lord, have we not prophesied in your name, cast out demons in your name, and done many wonders in your name?' And then I will declare to them, 'I never knew you; depart from me, you who practice lawlessness!' "**
>
> **Matthew 7:21-23 (NKJV)**

Jesus said, "Not every one that saith to me, 'Lord, Lord,' shall enter into the kingdom of Heaven: but he that doth the will of my FATHER who is in Heaven, he shall enter into the kingdom of Heaven. Many will say to me in that day: 'Lord, Lord, have not we prophesied in thy name, and cast out devils in thy name, and done many miracles in thy name?' And then will I profess unto them, 'I never knew you: depart from me, you that work iniquity.' " Matthew 7:21-23 (Douay-Rheims)

Jesus said, "Not everyone who says to me, 'Lord, Lord,' will enter the kingdom of Heaven, but only the one who does the will of my FATHER in Heaven. Many will say to me on that day, 'Lord, Lord, did we not prophesy in your name? Did we not drive out demons in your name? Did we not do mighty deeds in your name?' Then I will declare to them solemnly, 'I never knew you. Depart from me, you evildoers.' "
Matthew 7:21-23 (NAB)

Jesus' warning in Matthew 7:21-23 is followed by his definitions of who are wise and who are foolish.

Jesus defines a wise person:

"Therefore whoever hears these sayings of mine, and does them, I will liken him to a wise man [who built his home on a solid rock]." v24

*A wise person is a **doer** of God's Word!*

Jesus defines a foolish person:

"Now everyone who hears these sayings of mine, and does not do them, will be like a foolish man [who built his home on sand]." v25

*A foolish person is a **hearer** of God's Word!*

Prayer

FATHER, God of my brother Jesus Christ and God of my life and of all human life, hear this prayer from YOUR apostle's heart. FATHER, I have done what you have asked me to do. I have warned Christians in the <u>Book of Edward</u> that many of them will be headed towards Hell instead of Heaven for all the reasons that YOU gave me. Now, this book is finished and the <u>Seven End-Times Messages</u> have been delivered. I pray for all the Christian souls that are lost FATHER. I pray that all whom YOU desire to obtain the truth found in these books will find it. Have mercy on them as you gather up all righteous souls for YOUR kingdom. Many Christians have been falsely programmed by Satan's trinity doctrine designed to take the worship away from YOU and place it upon YOUR only begotten human Son Jesus. FATHER, grant everyone with a sincere heart the ability to fully understand YOUR Son Jesus. Grant them the ability to see clearly what YOUR Son Jesus taught us. Grant them the ability to fully understand YOUR Word. For every sincere heart and righteous soul, I ask for mercy on their confusion because of the false teaching they have been programmed with since 325 AD. Surely the people should not suffer for the evil teachings of Church leaders. Nevertheless, as my brother has taught me, THY will be done O' LORD! And it is surely true that vengeance belongs to YOU. Edward

Kyrie eleison[43]

Choose wisely whom you will believe!
Choose to believe Jesus!

Apostle Edward

Appendix A
A Real Salvation Prayer

OPENING PRAYER: FATHER God, let everyone who utters this prayer of salvation unto YOU, with a sincere heart, immediately feel the presence of YOUR Holy Spirit and equip them with the internal strength of conviction to stand tall for YOUR righteousness at all costs and even unto their own human death. Verily I say unto YOU that this is YOUR expectation of their [my] sincere heart. The Apostle Edward

INSTRUCTIONS: Pray out loud and offer up to God Almighty outstretched arms and the following prayer, on your knees, in the privacy of your prayer closet [private room, alone], and with your sincere heart. Verily I say unto you that your soul will see eternal life in Heaven upon the death of your earthly body if your heart is sincere with God to the point that your behavior turns to righteousness. Mark down the time, date and place of this gift of your heart to God and feel free to share this moment of time when you made a commitment to walk in God's ways with HIS priorities over your life.

PRAY: Heavenly FATHER, the only ONE and True God. YOU, who are also the FATHER and the only ONE and True God of my brother Jesus Christ whom YOU sent down as a living human sacrifice for the sins of all the humans in this earthly realm and world, hear this prayer from my sincere heart. This prayer comes from within the bowels of my spirit-soul and I fully understand that this is a one-way decision of my heart.
FATHER, I believe in YOUR only human begotten Son Jesus Christ. I believe that YOU sent Christ down to this earth and that he became the human being Jesus Christ [Yashua] in the flesh just like the flesh I have. I believe he had bones like I do, flesh like I do and blood like I do. I believe that his body on the cross was no different than any other human body on the cross. I acknowledge Jesus Christ is the Son of God; he is not God.

FATHER, I believe that he only spoke what YOU told him to say and that he only did what YOU told him to do. I believe that he was the final and perfect blood sacrifice for the forgiveness of the sins of mankind. FATHER I believe that includes my sins.

LORD, I fully acknowledge that by accepting Jesus Christ as my personal savior and brother that I am inviting his perfect spirit into my life to share this earthly body with me. Along with his spirit, I understand that you will also give me YOUR Holy Spirit and that YOU also will dwell within me.

I believe that the end result of my sincere acceptance of this gift of YOUR Son is the Oneness that I will share with YOU and him. Christ has taught me that I might live in perfect Oneness, Peace and Joy with YOU and him. O LORD, this is truly the sincere desire of my heart. I no longer want to be spiritually alone.

Therefore, I accept the precious gift of YOUR Son Jesus Christ and I repent of my past sins and sincerely regret every thought, action, behavior or anything that was displeasing unto YOU. I understand that with the precious gift of YOUR Son, YOU expect me to live a righteousness life the rest of my days on this earth.

Such a life entails living up to YOUR expectations and obeying what YOU and YOUR Son taught us in Holy Scripture. LORD, I acknowledge that I cannot be perfect in and of myself. I realize that to be like Christ requires that I "practice" righteousness and that I avoid sin to the best of my ability. I acknowledge that to continue willfully to sin is a tacit rejection of the gift of Jesus.

I also acknowledge, FATHER, that there will be unintentional and unknown sins that will come in my life. I understand that YOU and Christ will cover those types of sin and function as a guide in my life to keep me on the narrow path to Heaven.

FATHER, I acknowledge that YOUR Son is not a free pass on sins like so many Christians believe. Therefore, when I realize I have sinned against YOU in any way, I promise to confess that sin immediately and to keep a short list of my missteps with YOU. I know YOU are faithful to forgive under such conditions, but I also realize that if any life is filled with such confessions that it will be a testimony of an insincere heart. I recognize YOUR instructions in Ezekiel 18 and that Jesus has not altered YOUR criteria for punishing sinners. Therefore, keep me under YOUR wings O God and give me a pure heart unto YOU.

Having said this, FATHER, I pray that you will dwell within me and help me to be the man [or woman] that you want me to be. I ask all of this in the name of Jesus Christ whom I confess with my mouth that he came in the flesh as YOUR only begotten SON. I acknowledge with my heart that YOU expect righteousness, a new life with changed behavior; behavior that glorifies YOU.

FATHER, help me to be an instrument of YOUR will even as Christ was such an instrument. Let this day be the first day of the rest of my life and help me to put away all offensive behavior and sin, which YOU hate. In the name of YOUR only begotten and beloved human Son Jesus, I pray. AMEN

Date and Time of Prayer: _____

Place of Prayer: _____

I First Told To: _____

_____

Testimony: _____

_____

Appendix B
Baptism Doctrine

THE QUESTION

An Internet email writer asks Apostle Edward: "What is your doctrine on baptism? Do you believe that it is necessary to be baptized in order to go to Heaven?"

Dear Seeker,

This is a very deep question. I will do my best to answer it faithfully in a way that honors God and His Holy Scripture.

DOCTRINE

I believe in baptism by immersion as an "outward expression of a new heart, which is now set aside for God." In effect, such a water baptism declares to all you know [and to the world] that you are indeed a part of God's kingdom [and you are indeed headed towards a heavenly kingdom].

COMMENTARY & STUDY

In Ephesians 4:5 we read: "There is one Lord, one faith, one baptism." However, in Acts 19:3-4 we see the question posed: "Into what then were you baptized?" The answer: "Into John's baptism." John's baptism was one of "repentance for the remission of sins." See Mark 1:4. Explicit in Acts 19:3-4 is the reality that there was more than one type of baptism.

John the Baptist offered the proposition of a "real God, Heaven and Hell and thus a real reason for sincere repentance" to the people. It is clear in God's Word that any such sincere repentance [of the heart] would yield salvation or eternal life. Thus baptism, in this instance by John, leads to eternal life in Heaven. John's baptism is not well understood in Christianity, which has perverted the intent of God's Holy Word and the Gospel of Christ.

However, Ephesians 4:5 refers to another and second baptism. It is the baptism of Romans 6:4: "Therefore we were buried with him [Christ Jesus] through baptism into death, that just as Christ was raised from the dead by the glory of the FATHER, even so we should walk in newness of life."

Anyone who accepts Jesus Christ "in their heart" has indeed accepted the reality of God and has achieved a baptism of the Holy Spirit [a baptism unto death and resurrection in Christ]. This results in the indwelling of God, His Son and the Spirit of truth that allows you to walk in a "newness of life." It gives you the strength to stand tall, firm and unwavering for God's truth in the simple language of the Holy Bible. Such a person now manifests the kingdom of God from within outward into the world around them. Even though, at this point, there may not have been a water baptism.

Baby baptism means virtually nothing because at the age of accountability [about 12 years old], each individual will have to make his or her choice as to which side he or she is on. No one can make this choice for another soul.

It took 10 years, after God touched my heart, for me to get baptized by immersion. It was a wonderful moment in time for me as it had bothered my spirit for a long time. Perhaps out of the misdirection of Christian theology and not fully understanding God's Holy Word. Or, perhaps out of the desire of my heart to proclaim that "I belong to God." Or, perhaps out of verses like Acts 10:47 indicating I could be baptized "having already received the Holy Spirit" and Acts 8:37 since "I believed with all my heart."

The verse that was my spiritual testimony at the time of my water baptism was Acts 22:15-16: "For you will be HIS witness to all men of what you have seen and heard. 'And now why are you waiting? Arise and be baptized, and wash away your sins, calling on the name of the LORD.' "

And now, Edward, why are *you* waiting? I knew where my heart was and the book of Acts indicated to my spirit that it was a special privilege to get baptized by immersion having met all of God's 'heart' criteria to ... make an outward declaration of the faith that was inside of my heart!

CASE 1: Anyone who is baptized by immersion and repents unto God for his or her sins will be saved and enter into eternal life. Assuming they then walk a godly life. This is true even without them having accepted Christ since they have already "accepted God."

CASE 2: Anyone who accepts Christ accepts God and, if Christ is within them, they will walk in the newness of life through a baptism of the Holy Spirit. This is true even if they have not been water baptized by immersion. Assuming they then walk a godly life and are "truly repentant."

This baptism doctrine fully recognizes all of God's Word. When you study Ezekiel 18, you will understand Case 1. It is consistent with the Gospel of Christ, which is "to repent and be saved." Many Christians no longer have this perspective of repentance. It is a critical part of salvation. Repentance leads to righteousness. Righteous people belong to God!

Case 2 is also consistent with God's Word. God has offered us a different dynamic with HIS Son. Plus, HE has provided some spiritual help that we can internalize through Christ: the indwelling of HIS Holy Spirit abundantly. Case 2 is consistent with Romans 10:9-10, which spells out what is required for salvation through Christ. Water baptism is not a part of the criteria Paul outlined, because his criteria, results in a baptism of your spirit-soul and also a committed heart. As such, you have accepted God's Spirit via Christ. It is a 'Spirit' baptism. Both baptisms require the total surrendering of your heart and life in obedience to God. Do either and HIS Spirit will confirm to your spirit-soul that you are indeed saved unto eternal life.

The Apostle Edward

"THE LORD OUR GOD IS ONE!" Deut 6:4

Appendix C
Thomas' Exclamation

> "Then [Jesus] said to Thomas, 'Put your finger here and see my hands, and bring your hand and put it into my side, and do not be unbelieving, but believe.' Thomas answered and said to him, 'My Lord and my God!' Jesus said to him, 'Have you come to believe because you have seen me? Blessed are those who have not seen and have believed.' Now Jesus did many other signs in the presence of (his) disciples that are not written in this book. But these are written that you may (come to) believe that Jesus is the Messiah, the Son of God, and that through this belief you may have life in his name."
>
> John 20:27-31 (NAB)

Thomas answered and said to Jesus: "My Lord and my God!" v28

So desperate are Trinitarian believers to rationalize the false doctrine of the trinity, that they will take verses out of context, ignore prior teachings of Jesus and in the process, make our Lord Jesus Christ a complete liar. A mere eleven verses earlier we read:

> **Jesus said to her, "Stop holding on to me, for I have not yet ascended to the Father. But go to my brothers and tell them, 'I am going to my FATHER and your FATHER, to my God and your God.'"**
>
> John 20:17 (NAB)

In our modern vernacular, Thomas' statement would be most properly interpreted as meaning, "O' my God, its true, its Jesus!" Thomas does not say: "Jesus is God!" as so many think he has. Did Jesus lie to us eleven verses earlier in the same chapter? If not, then how can anyone teach or believe Apostle Thomas would verbalize such apostasy? If you continue reading after Thomas' exclamation, we see that that "these words are written" in the book of John so that you may ...

"Come to believe that Jesus is the Messiah, the Son of God!" v31

Or how about, **"Peace to you! As the FATHER has sent me, I also send you." v21**

And, then Jesus breathed on them saying, **"Receive the Holy Spirit." v22**

Thomas was not with them when the other Apostles received the Holy Spirit or the Spirit of Truth. However, eight days later, Thomas was present when Jesus returned. This is the context for Thomas' exclamatory statement in John chapter 20. Yet, there is so much more context when it comes to what the apostles were taught. Jesus made it plain to all of his disciples that he was not God.

In Jesus' prayers to God [earlier in John 17], he told our FATHER that he had taught the disciples HIS Word and that they remained faithful to God's Word. Listen carefully,

> **Jesus, while praying to God said: "I revealed YOUR name to those whom YOU gave me out of the world. They belonged to YOU, and YOU gave them to me, and they have kept YOUR word. Now they know that everything YOU gave me is from YOU, because the words YOU gave to me I have given to them, and they accepted them and truly understood that I came from YOU, and they have believed that YOU sent me." John 17:6-8 (NAB)**

So, Jesus told God that his disciples:

A) Had God's name [Yahweh] revealed to them;
B) Had kept God's Word;
C) Knew God gave everything to Jesus;
D) Accepted Jesus' teachings as words from God;
E) Truly understood Jesus was the Son of God, the Christ, who came from God;
F) Believed that God [Yahweh] had sent Jesus.

I feel a righteous indignation swelling up into my body and I feel like literally *SCREAMING AT THE TOP OF MY LUNGS*, "Why do people make Jesus a liar by claiming 'Thomas worshipped Jesus and identified him as God?'" The Apostle Thomas knew better than to do such a thing! How do we know? Jesus teaches us that the apostles "knew who God was!" I could go deeper and cite many other verses, but what is the point? Isn't this enough? Can't you simply accept the teachings of Jesus as truth?

> **"If anyone teaches otherwise and does not consent to wholesome words, even the words of our Lord Jesus Christ, and to the doctrine which is according to godliness, he is proud, knowing nothing, but is obsessed with disputes and arguments over words, from which come envy, strife, reviling, evil suspicions." 1 Timothy 6:3-4 (NKJV)**

I tell you to accept the teachings of our Lord Jesus Christ and stop making him out to be a liar by contradicting him or twisting his words. Meditate on 1 Timothy 6:3-4 if you don't get it. You must accept the teachings of Jesus if you want to understand Scripture. If you don't agree and consent to the teachings of Jesus, "you know nothing!" Surely God will repay every teacher who misleads others about the teachings of our Lord Jesus Christ.

Remember John 20:17? Where Jesus identifies our God? Then why not simply …

Accept Jesus' teaching that the identity— Of his and our <u>God</u>, *is actually just* <u>the FATHER</u>!

Appendix D
Catholics & The Bible

I recently wrote a woman I love saying, "Choose either Catholicism or the Bible. I now realize from many days of studies that there are too many areas in which the Catholic Church actually teaches against Holy Scripture. Had I realized this aspect of Catholicism, I would not have troubled you with Scripture. Honestly, I had no idea of the depths of the teachings against Scripture within the Catholic Church. I didn't even fully appreciate what all the fuss was about different faiths. I knew that some Christians believed the Bible and others didn't. It was to those who did not believe the Bible, but called themselves a Christian that God has me writing. I now realize the Catholic Church holds Scripture in lower esteem than its own man-made declarations, but I did not fully appreciate this until after our discussions and a further study of Catholicism."

Catholics get into a lot of difficulty trying to explain away easy to understand Scripture. And, of course, the Catholic Church gives them many reasons to explain away Scripture. The word of God may not speak to some Catholics, because the Church subordinates HIS Word in favor of its own traditions and Papal teachings. Yet, can the Bible be discounted and ignored with impunity? No, it can't. Without any further thoughts, I want to share a testimony from David Briggs, an ex-Catholic. His testimonial website contains resources for all Christians. Catholics in particular will find a lot of information including Catholic history that they may not know. I recommend this site to further understand the Catholic faith. The question is: "Does Catholicism teach the Bible? The Catholic *New American Bible*?" Of course, if you are a Catholic and have read this far, the answer should be self-evident. Catholicism subordinates God's Word and holds its own man-made traditions and Papal teachings in higher esteem and greater reverence than the basis of their faith, which should be Holy Scripture. Let David Riggs explain it from his perspective.

Why I Left The Catholic Church
David Riggs Testimonial

Following are my notes on a sermon that I preached shortly after I was converted from the Catholic Church back in 1962. It was the first sermon that I preached.

Introduction:

I came from a large, devout Catholic family of twelve children. I attended Trinity High School in Louisville, Kentucky. At the time of my intense Scriptural study, I had two brothers who were enrolled in Catholic seminaries studying to be priests. I also want to state I did not leave the Catholic Church because of some evil that I had done or that was done to me. I left the Catholic Church because I came to believe that it was contrary to the Bible. This I will endeavor to show in this study.

The First Reason: Catholics Do Not Have The Right Attitude Toward The Truth.

To illustrate what I mean by this, I will explain the difference in the two sides. Those with the right attitude toward the truth are always willing to test what they teach with others. They invite those of opposite views to work together for truth and unity. They appreciate when those who differ with them point out where they think they are wrong. They have everything thoroughly tested, studying arguments both for and against, looking at both sides of the question.

Those with the wrong attitude toward the truth are not willing to test what they teach in fair and open discussion, privately or publicly. They do not invite others to point out where they think they are wrong, and do not appreciate when others try to do so. They won't allow their members to hear both sides of an issue, and especially they don't want them to examine opposing arguments.

Hopefully, one can now understand what I mean when I said [that] Catholics do not have the right attitude toward the truth. Catholics are not allowed, and especially are not encouraged to hear both sides regarding truth and error. They are not to read books, which differ from their doctrine. Thus, they are encouraged by the clergy to be closed minded to anything, which differs from Catholicism. We ask, "Why don't Catholic officials encourage their members to examine opposing Scriptural teaching?" False teachers have learned that when truth and error are examined side by side, some begin to see the truth. False teachers are afraid of being exposed and of losing their members.

The Second Reason: The Bible Is The Only All-Sufficient Guide To Salvation, But The Catholic Church Teaches That It Is Not.

The Catholic *Catechism For Adults* on page 52 says, "Can you learn to save your soul just by reading the Bible? No, because certain things in the Bible can be misunderstood, and because the Bible does not have everything God taught." Notice that the first part of their answer to "Can you learn to save your soul just by reading the Bible?" is, "No." However, their own translations of the Bible teaches the opposite. All Scriptural quotations that I will be giving are from Catholic translations. 2 Tim. 3:15-17 says, "And because from thy infancy thou hast known the Holy Scriptures, which can instruct thee to salvation, by faith which is Christ Jesus. All scripture, inspired of God, is profitable to teach, to reprove, to correct, to instruct in justice, that the man of God may be perfect, furnished to every good work." Thus, the apostle Paul by the inspiration of God says to Timothy "thou hast known the holy scriptures, which can instruct thee to salvation" and make you "perfect, furnished to every good work."

Rom. 1:16 says, "For I am not ashamed of the gospel. For it is the power of God unto salvation to everyone that believeth, to the Jew first, and to the Greek. James 1:21 says, "...With meekness receive the ingrafted word, which is able to save you souls." Consequently, the word contained in the Bible is able to save our souls.

The next part of the answer in the Catechism to the question, "Can you learn to save your soul just by the Bible?" is, "No, because certain things in the Bible can be misunderstood..." They are implying that the Bible cannot be understood. John A. O'Brien, the Catholic author of the book, "*The Faith of Millions*," is much more expressive when he says on page 152, "The Bible is not a clear and intelligible guide to all..." The book, "*The Faith of Millions*" was given to me before my conversion by my older brother Norman who was at the time a student at St. Meinrad Seminary, St. Meinrad, Indiana.

The apostle Paul said we could understand what he wrote. "If yet, you have heard of the dispensation of the grace of God which is given me towards you: how that, according to revelation, the mystery has been made known to me, as I have written above in few words; as you reading, may understand my knowledge in the mystery of Christ." (Eph. 3:2-4). Paul said the mystery had been made [known] to him by the revelation of God. He then showed that he was writing it e.g., "as I have written above in few words" (in the chapters prior to this) and "as you reading, may understand my knowledge in the mystery of Christ." In other words, when we read what he wrote, we can understand what he understood. Paul also said, "For we write nothing to you that you do not read and understand" (2 Cor. 1:13) and "Therefore do not become foolish, but understand what the will of the Lord is" (Eph. 5:17). Thus, the inspired writers taught that we most certainly could understand the Scriptures.

The last part of the answer given in the Catechism to the question, "Can you learn to save your soul just by reading the Bible?" was "No because the Bible does not have everything God taught." *The Faith of Millions*, on pages 153-154 says, "The Bible does not contain all the teaching of the Christian religion, nor does it formulate all the duties of its members." The Scriptures contain everything that is necessary to equip the man of God for every good work (2 Tim. 3:16-17). There is not a solitary good work that the Christian can do which is not provided in the Scriptures. The Scriptural proof they give for the Bible not containing everything God taught, is John 20:30. It says, "Many other signs also did Jesus in the sight of his disciples, which are not written in this book." (See *Catechism For Adults*, p. 10).

In John 20:30, John simply said that Jesus did many other signs (miracles), which he did record. Notice, though, what John says in the next verse, "But these are written that you may believe that Jesus is the Christ, the Son of God, and that believing you may have life in his name." Thus, the apostle clearly shows that he wrote sufficient things to produce the faith, which brings life in the name of Jesus. Life in the name of Jesus refers to eternal life and it is obtained by belief in the things written by the inspired writers.

We freely admit that the Scriptures do not contain everything Jesus did. John said, "There are, however, many other things that Jesus did; but if every one of these would be written, not even the world itself, I think, could hold the books that would have to be written." (John 21:25). Although we do not have everything Jesus did, we do have every *necessary* thing. We have enough to give us life in his name.

Catholic officials follow up their claim (that we cannot understand the Bible) by stating that one can get the true meaning only from the Catholic Church. The *Catechism For*

Adults on page 10 says, "How can you get the true meaning of the Bible? You can get it only from God's official interpreter, the Catholic Church." The Catholics have no passages, which mention an official interpreter, and, thus, they try to support their claim through human logic and reasoning. Anytime men do such, it amounts to nothing more than human philosophy rather than Scriptural proof. The Bible says, "Let God be true, but every man a liar..." (Rom. 3:4). It also warns, "See to it that no one deceives you by philosophy and vain deceit, according to human traditions, according to the elements of the world and not according to Christ." (Col. 2:8).

The doctrine of the "infallible interpreter" implies that God did not make HIMSELF clear. It implies that God gave us a revelation that still needs revealing. Did God fail in HIS attempt to give man a revelation? Do the Catholic officials want us to believe they can express God's will more clearly than God HIMSELF? We believe that God made the mind of man and is fully capable of addressing man in words which man can understand.

The Third Reason: Christ Did Not Make His Church Infallible As The Catholic Church Teaches.

The Catholic writers try to teach that the church could never go into error and is preserved from error. The *Catechism For Adults* on page 56 says, "Why can't the Catholic Church ever teach error? Because Jesus promised to be always with His Church to protect it from error." The book, "*My Catholic Faith,*" which is based heavily on materials from the *Baltimore Catechism*, was given to me by my father not long after I was converted. I think his intentions were that somehow it would cause me to return to the Catholic Church. It says on page 144, "Jesus Christ promised to preserve the Church from error." On page 145, it says, "Jesus Christ commanded all men to listen to and obey the Church, under pain of damnation. If his Church can teach error then he is responsible for the error, by commanding all to obey." On page 54 the *Catechism For Adults* says, "Does everyone have to obey the Catholic Church? Yes, because she alone has the authority of Jesus to rule and to teach." It is easy to see that Catholics have the authority in the wrong place. The authority is not in the body, but in the Head (Eph. 1:22-23; Col. 1:18). The ruling is not in the kingdom, but in the King (Heb. 7:1-2; Rev. 1:5-6). The authority is in not in the church, but in Christ (Matt. 28:18; 1 Pet. 3:22). The church is not the Savior, but simply the body of the saved (Acts 2:47; Eph. 5:22-24).

There are many passages in the New Testament, which reveal that the church would not be preserved from error. Acts 20:17, 28-30; 2 Pet. 2:1-3; 1 Tim. 4:1-3; 2 Tim. 4:3-4; 2 Thess. 2:3-11. We see from these passages that there was to come a great falling away from the truth. In Acts chapter twenty we learn that perverse things would come from the bishops of the church. Peter said (2 Pet. 2) that false teachers would arise among you (working from within) and there would be *many* who would follow them. Paul [tells] us (2 Thess. 2) that the apostasy was already underway, "for the mystery of iniquity is already at work..." (Verse 7). It started in Paul's day and was to continue until the second coming of Christ. He added, "...Whom the Lord Jesus will slay with the breath of his mouth and will destroy with the brightness of his coming." (Verse 8).

We cannot harmonize that which the inspired apostles said (there shall arise false teachers among you) with that which the Catholic writers say (shall be preserved from error). Furthermore, we call your attention to the fact that the characteristics of the departing group are identical with those of the Catholic Church. Everyone knows that the Catholic Church has forbidden its people to eat meat on Friday and at the present it forbids some from marriage. Also, the only way for the wicked one to last from Paul's day to the second coming of Christ is to have a continual succession. It could not be some wicked person of the past because he will not be here for the Lord to slay when he comes. Furthermore, it could not be ones in the future because their iniquity would not have started in Paul's day. It must, therefore, be a continual succession from the beginning until now. The Catholic Church is the only group, which perfectly fits the apostles' description of the great apostasy.

The seven short epistles to seven churches of Asia in the book of Revelation reveal the relationship the church sustains to Christ (See Rev. chapters 2 and 3; see especially 2:1-5, 12-14, 18-20; 3:1-3, 14-15). Those verses plainly reveal that when a church continues in Christ's word, it keeps its identity as his church, but when it fails to abide in HIS word; it is not longer regarded as his church. Also, they reveal that Christ did not establish His church as one that could never fall into error, because some of those churches went into error. Someone might say that the passages in Revelation referred to the various parishes or congregations rather than the whole church. It is true that the verses were speaking of local churches; nevertheless, the same principle that applied to them relates to the whole church. The Lord does not have a rule for one congregation, which is not equally applicable to all. If one church is rejected for embracing error, all others who likewise embrace error are rejected. The early churches had to earnestly contend for the faith, and to continually be on guard against error arising from within. The doctrine of an "infallible church" causes the Catholic Church to fail in this. The Catholic Church is a church, which neither recognizes nor corrects its errors.

The Fourth Reason: Christ Did Not Make Peter A Pope.

In the books of men, the following titles are commonly used with reference to a man: "Pope," "Holy Father," "Vicar of Christ," "Sovereign Pontiff." All of these are titles that rightly belong only to the Lord Jesus Christ and to God the FATHER. There is not a single instance in the Scriptures where any of the above titles are applied to a man. The term, "Holy Father" is used only once in the entire Bible, and it is used by Jesus in addressing God the FATHER. (John 17:11). Among the above titles is the bold assertion that the Pope is the "Vicar of Christ." A "vicar" is "One serving as a substitute or agent; one authorized to perform the functions of another in higher office." (Webster). When one searches the Bible from cover to cover, he finds only one passage, which gives an indication of a Vicar of Christ or God. It is 2 Thess. 2:3-4 and is worded as follows: "Let no one deceive you in any way, for the day of the Lord will not come unless the apostasy comes first, and the man of sin is revealed, the son of perdition, who opposes and is exalted above all that is called God, or that is worshipped, so that he sits in the temple of God and gives himself out as if he were God."

Some religionists today advocate that man is saved by faith only. However, there is only one passage in the entire Bible that has the words "faith" and "only" together and it says, "not by faith only" (James 2:24). The Catholics today speak of the Pope as vicar, taking the place of God [], yet there is only one passage in the entire Bible, which speaks of a man doing such and it calls him "the man of sin."

James Cardinal Gibbons, a Catholic Archbishop said, "Jesus our Lord, founded but one Church, which he was pleased to build on Peter. Therefore, any church that does not recognize Peter as its foundation stone is not the Church of Christ, and therefore cannot stand, for it is not the work of God." (*The Faith of Our Fathers*, p. 82). The apostle Paul said, "For other foundation no one can lay, but that which has been laid, which is Christ Jesus" (1 Cor. 3:11). There is no other foundation but Christ! Therefore, any church, which does not recognize Christ alone as the foundation stone, cannot be the church of Christ.

Catholic writers often speak of "the primacy of Peter" and "the primacy of the Pope." However, Col. 1:18, speaking of Christ, says, "And he is the head of the body, the church, who is the beginning, the first-born from the dead; that in all things he may hold the primacy..." Thus, with reference to the authority in the church, the Lord Jesus Christ holds the primacy *in all things*. This leaves nothing for the Pope!

Catholics claim that the Pope is the visible head of the church. The Catholic book *Answer Wisely*, by Martin J. Scott says on p. 49, "The pope, therefore, as vicar of Christ, is the visible head of Christ's kingdom on earth, the Church, of which Christ himself is the invisible head." The book *Father Smith Instructs Jackson*, by John F. Noll and Lester J. Fallon, on page 42 says, "According to the will of Christ, all its members profess the same faith, have the same worship and Sacraments, and are united under the one and same visible head, the Pope." Catholic officials always use the word "visible" no doubt thinking that it removes the thought of the Pope standing in opposition to the headship of Christ, and removes the apparent problem of having a church with two heads.

Nonetheless, the Scriptures nowhere teach the idea of a visible and invisible head. Jesus said, "All authority *in Heaven and on earth* has been given to me." (Matt. 28:18). Luke 17:20-21 says, "And on being asked by the Pharisees, 'When is the kingdom of God coming?' [Jesus] answered and said to them, the kingdom of God comes unawares. Neither will they say, 'Behold, here it is,' or 'Behold, there it is.' For behold the kingdom of God is within you." The kingdom of God is a spiritual kingdom and therefore needs only a spiritual head or king.

Eph. 5:23-25 shows that Christ is the only head of the church. "Let wives be subject to their husbands as to the Lord; because a husband is the head of the wife, just as Christ is head of the Church, being himself savior of the body. But just as the Church is subject to Christ, so also let the wives be to their husbands in all things." Consequently, the wife is subject to her husband as the church is to Christ. Just as the wife is subject to only one head--her husband, the church is subject to only one head--Christ. Just as the husband does not send a substitute to rule over his wife, Christ does not authorize a substitute to rule over his bride, the church.

Catholics often use the expression, "One fold and one shepherd" to sustain the doctrine of the papacy. (See *Catechism For Adults*, p. 59). They teach that the "one shepherd" is the Pope and the "one fold" represents the Catholic Church. Hear what Jesus said about it: "I am the good shepherd. The good shepherd lays down his life for his sheep...I am the good shepherd, and I know mine and mine know me, even as the FATHER knows me and I know the FATHER; and I lay down my life for my sheep. And other sheep I have that are not of this fold. Them also I must bring and they shall hear my voice, and there shall be one fold and one shepherd." (John 10:11, 14-16). Jesus is that one good shepherd. If one can understand that one and one equals two, he can understand this. If one is subject to Christ as the one shepherd — that's one. If one is subject to the Pope as the one Shepherd — that's two!

The church is often compared to the human body in the Scriptures. The members of the church are represented as the various parts of the body. Christ is always said to be the head. (See 1 Cor. 12:12-27; Eph. 1:22-23; 4:15-16). Our question is: "What part of the body is the Pope?" Also, "How does one get the idea of a sub-head into the body?" One of the greatest arguments against the primacy of Peter is the fact that the apostles had an argument among themselves as to which of them should be the greatest. Luke 22:24-26 says, "Now there arose a dispute among them, which of them was reputed to be the greatest. But [Jesus] said to them, 'the kings of the Gentiles lord it over them, and they who exercise authority over them are called benefactors. But not so with you. On the contrary, let him who is greatest among you become as the youngest, and him who is chief as the servant'." The very fact that the apostles had an argument among themselves shows they did not understand that Peter was to be prince. Also, the occasion of the argument was the night of the betrayal--the last night of the Lord's earthly ministry--and yet the apostles still did not understand that Christ had given Peter a position of primacy. The Lord settled the argument, not by stating that he had already made Peter head, but by declaring that the Gentiles have their heads, "But not so with you." Thus, Jesus very plainly taught that no one would occupy any such place as a benefactor (or Pope) to exercise authority over the others.

This testimonial is presented to help Catholics understand their attitudes towards God's Word and why they may not trust in the Bible's simple language as God's truth. David Riggs testimonial can also be found online at http://www.bible.ca/cath-why-I-left.htm. A second testimonial follows David's at this URL. The main study web site for additional study of Christianity is http://www.bible.ca/. (URL stands for universal resource locator or simply web address in Internet terminology.)

Note: The above testimonial has some minor editing for ease of reading and compliance with the small caps protocol used to identify God in Scripture. Fair use in copyright law is claimed for presenting the above testimonial and its author has not been contacted. The Apostle Edward does not agree with other information contained at the main study web site. The site has its own trinity rationalization. Overall, however, the main study web site is a good resource with in depth information for studying Christian history and its belief systems. Its section on Catholicism is substantial and broad in scope.

Notes

1 — (1611) *The Authorized King James Version* (KJV). <u>Comment</u>: The KJV is in the public domain in the United States and is therefore freely used and quoted by many people. Also, anyone can freely publish the KJV Bible.

2 — (1982) *Holy Bible, New King James Version* (NKJV). Nashville, Tennessee: Thomas Nelson, Inc. Copyright © 1979, 1980, 1982. <u>Comment</u>: The NKJV is an update to the KJV and closely parallels the KJV text. In the author's opinion, the NKJV Bible is an excellent way to enjoy the KJV without getting entangled in trying to comprehend its archaic and outdated English. See chapter 6 for a discussion of the errors found in the KJV.

3 — (1987) *The Amplified Bible* (AMP). La Habra, California: The Zondervan Corporation and the Lockman Foundation.

4 — (1901) *American Standard Bible* (ASB).

5 — (1970) *New American Standard Bible* (NASB). New York, NY: Catholic Book Publishing Company. Copyright by the Confraternity of Christian Doctrine, Wash. DC.

6 — (1977) *New American Standard Bible* (NASB). New York, NY: Catholic Book Publishing Company. Copyright by the Confraternity of Christian Doctrine, Wash. DC.

7 — (1949) *Bible In Basic English* (BBE). Cambridge: The University Press, 1949. This Bible is in the Public Domain. It is downloadable and can be read online at http://www.o-bible.com/bbe.html.

8 — (1995) *Contemporary English Version* (CEV), Copyright by The American Bible Society, 1865 Broadway, New York, NY 10023.

9 — Darby, John Nelson. Public Domain, 1833. *Darby Bible* (DB).

10 — (1957) *New Catholic Edition of the Holy Bible* (Douay-Rheims), Copyright by Catholic Book Publishing Company, New York. *Note: the Old Testament is the Confraternity - Douay Version. The New Testament Confraternity Edition is a revision of the Challoner-Rheims Version.*

11— (1917) *Book of Enoch* (ENO). Richard Laurence 1883 Edition.

12 — (2001) *English Standard Version* (ESV), Copyright by Crossway Bibles, a division of Good News Publisher. Adapted from the Revised Standard Version of the Bible, copyright Division of Christian Education of the National Council of the Churches of Christ in the U.S.A.

13 — (1599) *The Geneva Bible* (GEN) is in the public domain and available online.

14 — (1978) *Good News Bible* (GN). Copyright by American Bible Society. New York: Thomas Nelson Publishers. Aka *"The Bible in Today's English Version;"* or, *"Today's English Version."*

15 — (1978) *Good News Bible; with Deuterocanonicals/Apocrypha* (GNA). Copyright by American Bible Society. New York: Thomas Nelson Publishers. Aka *"The Bible in Today's English Version; with Apocrypha."*

16 — (1995) *God's Word* (GW). Copyright by the Nations Bible Society. Database © 1997 by NavPress Software at www.WORDsearchBible.com.

17 — Mamre, Mechon (2002) *The Hebrew Bible in English according to the JPS 1917 Edition; HTML Version* (HEB). Internet: http://www.mechon-mamre.org.

18 — (1999) *Holman Christian Standard Bible* (HOL). Copyright © 2003, 2002, 2000, 1999 by Holman Bible Publishers.

19 — (1986) *International Children's Bible* (ICB). Copyright © 1986, 1988, 1999 by Tommy Nelson™, a division of Thomas Nelson, Inc.

20 — Berlin, Adele and Brettler, March Zvi (Editors) (2004) *Jewish Study Bible* (JSB). Jewish Publication Society, Tanakh Translation. Oxford, NY: Oxford University Press.

21 — (1971) *The Living Bible* (LIV). Wheaton, Illinois: Tyndale House Publishers.

22 — (1996) *Holy Bible, New Living Translation* (NLT). Wheaton, Illinois: Tyndale House Publishers.

23 — (1988) *Microbible* (MB). Copyright by Ellis Enterprises, Inc.

24 — (2003) *The Message* (MES). Copyright by Eugene H. Peterson, NavPress Publishing Group, P.O. Box 35001, Colorado Springs, CO 80935

25 — (1988) *Morris Literal Translation* (MLT). Copyright by Ellis Enterprises, Inc., Oklahoma City, OK. See "The Bible Library" software.

26 — Moffatt, James A. R. (1922, 1924, 1925, 1926, 1935, 1950, 1952 and 1954). *The Bible: James Moffatt Translation* (MOF). Final Edition used and Copyrighted in 1994 by Kregel Publications, Grand Rapids, Michigan.

27 — (1991) *New American Bible* (NAB), Copyright by the Confraternity of Christian Doctrine, 3211 Fourth Street, N.E., Washington D.C. 20017

28 — (2005) *The NET Bible, New English Translation*, Copyright 1996-2005, Biblical Studies Press, L.L.C., www.bible.org.

29 — (1984) *The Holy Bible, New International Version* (NIV). Copyright by International Bible Society. Published by Zondervan Bible Publishers.

30 — (1991) *The Holy Bible, New Century Version* (NCV). Aka *"The Everyday Bible."* Dallas, Texas: Word Publishing. <u>Comment</u>: Excellent modern English translation.

31 — (1985) *The New Jerusalem Bible* (NJB). Copyright by Darton, Longman & Todd Ltd and Doubleday, a division of Bantam Doubleday Dell Publishing.

32 — (1958) *Phillips New Testament Bible* (PNT). Copyright held by Harper Collins. Copyright Administrator, The Archbishops' Council, Church House, Great Smith Street, London SW1P 3AZ, Tel (UK): 020 7898 1451; Fax (UK) 020 7898 1449; e-mail copyright@c-of-e.org.uk. On the web at http://www.ccel.org/bible/phillips/JBPNT.htm

33 — (1989) *The Revised English Bible* (REB). Copyright by Oxford University Press and Cambridge University Press. <u>Comment</u>: The Revised English Bible is a revision of The New English Bible.

34 — (1952) *Revised Standard Version* (RSV). Copyright by Division of Christian Education of the National Council of Churches of Christ in the United States of America. Zondervan Publishing House.

35 — (1989) *New Revised Standard Version* (NRSV). Copyright by Division of Christian Education of the National Council of Churches of Christ in the United States of America. Zondervan Publishing House.

36 — (1981) *Simple English Translation, New Testament* (SET). Copyright by International Bible Translators, Inc.

37 — Scherman, Nosson and Zlotowitz, Meir (General Editors). (1996) *The Stone Edition, Tanach* (TAN). Brooklyn, New York: Mesorah Publications, Ltd.

38 — (1988) *Transliterated Bible* (TB). Copyright by Ellis Enterprises, Inc.

39 — Webster, Noah. Public Domain, 1833. *Webster's Bible* (WEB).

40 — Wesley, John. Public Domain, 1755. *Wesley New Testament* (WES).

41 — Clarke, J. Public Domain, 1909. *Weymouth's New Testament* (WEY).

42 — Young, Robert. Public Domain, 1898. *Young's Literal Translation* (YLT).

43 — "Kyrie eleison" is Greek and means "O' LORD have mercy." This phrase is used and sung in some Catholic Masses and appears as: Kýrie, eléison; Christé, eléison; Kýrie, eléison. "Lord, have mercy; Christ, have mercy; Lord, have mercy." It is usually sung three times as an allusion to the trinity.

Notice: Fair use under copyright laws are claimed for all the verses cited from the above bibles that are not in the public domain. Due to the scholarly nature of this religious book, the capitalization protocol deployed by its author to properly identify God in all Scripture, and the controversial nature of the trinity doctrine, no permissions have been sought from copyright holders. Readers are referred back to the original Bible works for the original capitalization of the words used within cited verses.

Index

Ability to reason with God
   Isaiah 1:18, vii
Abortion, vii
Adore
   Only Yahweh, 7
All Scripture
   Inspired by God, viii
Angels, Like
   Matthew 22:29-30, 84
Antichrist
   Denies Jesus only human, 15
   Nine teachings of, 15
   Teaches against Christ's humanity, 15
Apostles' Creed
   Beliefs, 57
   Comments, 56
   Creed Statement, 55
   Does not ask you to believe Holy Spirit is God, 57
   Does not ask you to believe Jesus is God, 57
   Origin, 56
   Update for 2009, 58
Arius
   God the FATHER bishop, 71
Athanasian Creed
   Trinity Doctrine, 72
Athanasius
   Trinity bishop, 71
Authority
   1 Peter 3:22, 104
   All apostles equal as servants, 107
   All belongs to Jesus' alone, 106
   Colossians 1:18, 104
   Ephesians 1:22-23, 104
   In Christ and not Church, 104
   Jesus' and not Church, 104
   Luke 22:24-26, 107
   Matthew 28:18, 104, 106
   Peter's not primacy, 107

Baptism Doctrine, 97
Baptize
   Holy Spirit baptism, 81
   In name of Jesus, 80
   John's water baptism, 81
Be Still
   To know God, 44
Bible
   Easy to program those ignorant of Scripture, 4
   Pick one up and study it, 3
   Reason Church doesn't want you to read, 4
Bible Definitions, iv

Bibles
   All over 98% in agreement, 13
   Have some nuances, 13
   Scribes have altered a few verses, 13
Bible Study
   Safe, 13
   Three or more bibles, 13
Bible Text
   Contains doctrine, 2
   Errant verses, 2
   Some translations skew Scripture, 2
Bible Verses
   1 Corinthians 3:11, 106
   1 Corinthians 3:16, 44
   1 Corinthians 8:3-6, 13, 34
   1 Corinthians 8:6, xi, 46, 76, 80
   1 Corinthians 8:6-7, 45
   1 Corinthians 8:7, 45, 47
   1 Corinthians 10:1-4, 24
   1 Corinthians 12:12-27, 107
   1 Corinthians 15:34, 74
   1 John 4:3, 35
   1 John 4:18, 79
   1 John 5:5, 25
   1 John 5:20, ix
   1 Peter 1:2, 47
   1 Peter 1:21-22, 35, 51
   1 Peter 3:22, 104
   1 Peter 4:17, 33
   1 Peter 22-25, 50
   1 Thessalonians 1:1, 46
   1 Thessalonians 4:15, 23
   1 Timothy 1:2, 47
   1 Timothy 2:5, 35
   1 Timothy 3:15, 78, 83
   1 Timothy 4:1-3, 104
   1 Timothy 6:3-4, 100
   1 Timothy 6:3-5, xi
   1 Timothy 6:3-6, ix
   2 Corinthians 1:13, ix, 103
   2 John 1:3, 47
   2 John 9, xi
   2 Peter 1:17, 47
   2 Peter 2, 104
   2 Peter 2:1-3, 104
   2 Thessalonians 1: 7-10, 28
   2 Thessalonians 2, 104
   2 Thessalonians 2:3-4, 105
   2 Thessalonians 2:3-11, 104
   2 Thessalonians 2:9-12, 31, 32
   2 Thessalonians 3:11-12, 86
   2 Timothy 1:2, 47

2 Timothy 1:7, 19
2 Timothy 3:12-15, 78
2 Timothy 3:15-17, 102
2 Timothy 3:16-17, viii, 103
2 Timothy 4:3-4, 32, 104
Acts 2:47, 104
Acts 3:26, ix
Acts 8:37, 98
Acts 10:47, 98
Acts 10:48, 80
Acts 11:16, 81
Acts 15:19, 48
Acts 17:24, 43
Acts 19:3-4, 97
Acts 20:17, 104
Acts 22:15-16, 98
Acts 26:17, 48
Colossians 1:12, 46
Colossians 1:15, 11, 35, 75
Colossians 1:18, 104, 106
Colossians 2:2, 46
Colossians 2:8, xi, 104
Deuteronomy 5:6-21, 3, 39
Deuteronomy 5:8-10, 39
Deuteronomy 6:4, 79, 98
Deuteronomy 12:32, 26
Deuteronomy 18:15-18, 21
Deuteronomy 18:22, 21
Enoch XXII [V]: 1-4, 56
Ephesians 1:2, 46
Ephesians 1:17, 35
Ephesians 1:22-23, 104, 107
Ephesians 3:2-4, 103
Ephesians 3:4, viii
Ephesians 4:5, 97
Ephesians 4:15-16, 107
Ephesians 5:17, viii, 103
Ephesians 5:22-24, 104
Ephesians 5:23-25, 106
Ephesians 6:23, 46
Exodus 20:1-17, 3, 39
Exodus 20:4-5, 39
Ezekiel 14:14, 74
Ezekiel 18, 98
Ezekiel 18:9, 74
Ezekiel 18:21, 74
Ezekiel 18:31, 74
Galatians 1:1, 46
Galatians 1:3, 46
Galatians 3:26, 20
Galatians 4:14, 23
Genesis 6:2-4, 24
Hebrews 1:1-6, 12
Hebrews 1:7-8 error, 12
Hebrews 1:9, 12
Hebrews 2:17, 15, 35, 88

Hebrews 3:1-2, 20
Hebrews 7:1-2, 104
Hebrews 10:9, 35
I Corinthians 14:22-23, 43
Isaiah 1:18, vii, 69
Isaiah 7:15, 34
Isaiah 40:5, 34
Isaiah 42:8, 34
Isaiah 44:8, 34
Isaiah 45:21, 34
Isaiah 57:15, 43
James 1:21, viii, 102
James 2:24, 106
Jeremiah 1:5, 22
Joel 2:32, 74
John 3:16, 74
John 4:24, 33
John 4:30, ix
John 4:34, x, 22
John 5:18, 79
John 5:19, 34
John 5:24, ix, 29, 74
John 5:24-30, 34
John 5:26, 74
John 5:30, ix, x, 22
John 5:36, ix
John 5:37, ix
John 5:38, ix
John 5:39-44, 34
John 6:27, 46
John 6:29, ix
John 6:30, ix
John 6:38, x, 22, 34
John 6:39, ix
John 6:39-54, 29
John 6:40, ix
John 6:44, ix
John 6:57, 35, 75
John 6:63, 49
John 7:16, ix, x, 22
John 7:18, ix
John 7:28, ix
John 7:29, ix
John 7:30, ix
John 8:16, ix
John 8:26, ix
John 8:31-32, 30
John 8:36, 86
John 8:42, ix, 35
John 8:44, 90
John 8:47, viii, 34, 90
John 8:54, 90
John 8:54-58, 51
John 8:58, 51, 79
John 9:4, ix, x, 22
John 10:11, 107

113

John 10:26, ix
John 11:42, ix
John 12:44, ix
John 12:45, ix
John 12:49, ix
John 13:16, ix, x
John 13:20, ix
John 14:1, 35
John 14:10, 44
John 14:16-17, 14
John 14:23, 14, 49
John 14:24, ix, x, 22
John 14:26, 14
John 14:28, 35, 57, 77
John 15:21, ix
John 16:5, ix
John 16:23-28, 24
John 16:28, 35
John 17:3, ix, x, 9, 34
John 17:6, 35
John 17:6-8, 100
John 17:8, ix
John 17:11, 105
John 17:11-12, 9
John 17:17, 30, 78
John 17:18, ix
John 17:21, ix
John 17:23, 49
John 17:25, ix
John 17:25-26, 9
John 20:17, xi, 8, 34, 76, 80, 99
John 20:20, 74
John 20:21, ix
John 20:27-31, 99
John 20:30, 103
John 21:25, 103
Jude 1:1, 47
Jude 1:6, 24
Luke 4:18, ix
Luke 4:43, ix, x
Luke 6:46, 74
Luke 9:48, ix
Luke 11:27-28, viii
Luke 17:20-21, 106
Luke 17:21-22, 44
Luke 20:36, 19
Luke 22:24-26, 107
Luke 23:43, 56
Luke 24:45, ix
Malachi 2:7-9, 6
Malachi 3:6, 80
Mark 1:4, 97
Mark 8:38, 75
Matthew 4:4, 4
Matthew 4:10, 7, 10
Matthew 5:9, 19

Matthew 5:17-18, 50
Matthew 5:20, 74
Matthew 7:13-14, 87, 91
Matthew 7:21, 58
Matthew 7:21-23, 50, 92, 93
Matthew 10:40, ix
Matthew 11:27, 17
Matthew 12:49-50, 20
Matthew 13:43, 74
Matthew 13:57, 21
Matthew 15:3, 5, 6
Matthew 15:3-9, 7
Matthew 15:24, ix
Matthew 16:13-18, 7
Matthew 17:5, ix
Matthew 19:17, 74
Matthew 22:29-30, 84
Matthew 22:40, 74
Matthew 28:18, 104, 106
Matthew 28:19, 79, 81
Numbers 23:19, 18, 34, 80
Philippians 2:5-12, 88
Philippians 2:6, 88, 89
Philippians 2:6-9, 35
Philippians 2:7, 88
Philippians 2:11, 46
Philippians 2:12, 84
Philippians 3:5-6, 77
Proverbs 8:22-31, 75
Proverbs 30:5-6, 34
Psalms 3:8, 74
Psalms 22:3, 43
Psalms 45:11, 44
Psalms 50:23, 74
Psalms 104:4, 34
Psalms 106:21, 34
Psalms 119:160, 30
Psalms 199:160, 78
Revelation 1:5-6, 104
Revelation 3:1, 35
Revelation 3:12, 10
Revelation 3:14, 11, 35, 75
Revelation 7:10, 74
Revelation 19:10, 10
Revelation 21:3, 34
Revelation 22:8-9, 10
Revelation 22:18-19, 26
Romans 1:3, 23
Romans 1:4, 23
Romans 1:16, 102
Romans 2:28-29, 84
Romans 3:4, 104
Romans 4:8, 74
Romans 5:15, 16
Romans 6:4, 97
Romans 6:22, 74

Romans 8:14, 19
Romans 8:19, 19
Romans 10:9-10, 98
Romans 10:10, 74
Romans 12:2, 86
Titus 1:4, 47
Titus 2:13-14 compared, 13
Titus 2:13-14 Douay-Rheims' error, 12
Titus 3:4-7, 86
Titus 3:6, 86
Wisdom 5:2, 74
Bible Verses - Tinkered
   Matthew 28:19, 81
Blessed
   Mary, viii
   More than Mary, viii
   Peter, 7
   Those who hear God's Word and obey it, viii
Book of Mormon
   Doctrinal errors, 2
Born Again
   1 Peter 22-25, 50
   Through God's living word - Bible, 50
Bound
   On earth and in Heaven, 7

C.S. Lewis
   Believed Jesus is God, 2
   Mere Christianity, 2
Capitalization Protocol, iii
Carved Images
   Catholics bow down to, 39
   Catholics make, 39
   Don't bow down to, 39
   Don't make any, 39
Carved Image Analysis
   What would God think, 42
Carved Image Table
   Different bibles compared, 41
Catholic
   Current Nicene Creed, 82
   Image rationalization, 44
   Profession of Faith 2009, 82
   Profession of Faith Scripture errors, 83
Catholic Bible
   Douay-Rheims, 4
   New American Bible, 4
Catholic Church
   Fallible, 105
   Holds Scripture in lower esteem than Church writings, 101
   Mother Church, 4
   Teaches against Catholic bibles, 76
   Worship rationale, 3

Catholic Creed
   Doesn't reflect God's truth, 83
   Negates God's commandments, 83
   Not of God, 83
   Reflects man-made doctrines, 83
   Teaches against Scripture, 83
Catholic Creed Denies
   1 Corinthians 8:6, 83
   1 Corinthians 12:13, 83
   1 John 1:3, 83
   1 Timothy 2:5, 83
   1 Timothy 3:15, 83
   Acts 1:4, 83
   Acts 8:37, 83
   Acts 1010:47-48, 83
   Acts 19:5, 83
   Acts 22:15-16, 83
   Colossians 1:15, 83
   Ephesians 4:1-6, 83
   Galatians 3:26, 83
   Hebrews 1:1, 83
   Hebrews 2:17, 83
   John 15:26, 83
   John 20:17, 83
   Luke 20:36, 83
   Matthew 4:10, 83
   Matthew 5:9
   Matthew 12:49-50, 83
   Matthew 21:31-32, 83
   Philippians 2:5-6, 83
   Proverbs 8:22-30, 83
   Revelation 1:1, 83
   Revelation 3:14, 83
   Revelation 22:9, 83
   Romans 6:4, 83
   Romans 8:14, 83
   Romans 8:19, 83
Catholicism
   Incompatible with Bible, 101
Catholic Mass
   Mystery of Christ, 3
   Outsider's view, 43
Catholics
   Bow before images, 3
Catholics & The Bible, 101
Choose
   To believe Jesus, 94
   Wisely, 94
Christianity
   Christian god forced on Roman empire, 66
   Christians persecuted for failure to worship images, 63
   Church fights dissent on God's identity, 66
   Constantine, 65
   Constantine convenes Nicea council in 325 to define God, 66

Christianity (Continued)
    Constantine gave Christians great favor, 65
    Constantine rejects trinity on deathbed, 70
    Constantine's power, 65
    Great Persecution of 303 AD, 64
    Heresy defined, 67
    Many pagan gods to compete with, 62
    Non-trinity believers persecuted/killed, 67
    Roman Catholic Church power grows, 68
    Romans resist a single all powerful God, 62
    Rome's relationship with early Christians, 63
    Rome starts making a distinction between Christians and Jews, 64
    Separated from Judaism, 63
    Started as Jewish sect, 63
    Tertullian coins trinity, 71
    The Beginnings, 62
    What is missing, vii
Christians
    Named, vii
    Programmed, vii
Christ's Teachings
    Those who do not obey are not of God, xi
Christ's Vengeance
    On those who do not know his God, 28
    On those who do not obey his teachings, 28
Church
    Body of the saved, 104
    Head is Christ, not the Pope, 107
    Must continue in God's Word, 105
    Not the Savior, 104
    Subject to Christ, 106
    Subject to God's Word, 106
Church, Body
    Ephesians 5:22-24, 104
Church, Fallible
    1 Timothy 4:1-3, 104
    2 Peter 2:1-3, 104
    2 Thessalonians 2:3-11, 104
    2 Timothy 4:3-4, 104
    Acts 20:17, 104
    Acts 28:32, 104
Church, False Teachers
    2 Peter 2, 104
Church, Head
    Ephesians 1:22-23, 107
    Ephesians 4:15-16, 107
Church Apostasy
    2 Thessalonians 2, 104
    2 Thessalonians 2:3-4, 105
Church Authority
    Jesus alone, not Pope, 106
Church Tradition
    Negates God's Word, 5
    Two soul stealing ones, 52

Coming Back
    Both Jesus and God, 12
Comma
    Changing Scripture with a comma, 12
Commandment, Second
    Deuteronomy 5:8-10, 39
    Exodus 20:4-5, 39
    Martin Luther missed Catholic deletion, 42
    Missing in Lutheran literature, 42
    Missing in Roman Catholic literature, 42
Commandments, Ten
    Catholic List, 42
    Deuteronomy 5:6-21, 39
    Exodus 20:1-17, 39
    Lutheran List, 42
Conclusion, 92
Constantine
    Built great Churches, 65
    Consolidates all power, 65
    Forces Christian trinity god on empire, 66
    Hostile to pagan gods, 66
    Rejects trinity god on deathbed, 70
    Start of his empire, 65
Copyright Notice, ii

David Riggs
    Catholic Testimonial, 101
    Christian history web site, 107
    Web site URL, 107
Deceiving Power
    2 Thessalonians 3:11-12, 86
Deception
    End-Times, 31
    Of those who perish, 31
    The greatest deception, 32
    Trinity doctrine, 31
Deception, End-Times
    2 Thessalonians 2:9-12, 31
Delusion
    God sends a strong one, 31
Doctrinal errors
    Book of Mormon, 2
    Douay-Rheims, 2
    New World Translation, 2
    Scripture, 2
Dogma
    Believed as true, 2
    Definition, 2
    Principle laid down by leaders as true, 2
Douay-Rheims
    Catholic Bible, 4
    Doctrinal errors, 2

Edward
    Apostles' Creed Update, 58
    God asks of him, 4

Edward (Continued)
- I and the FATHER are one, 49
- Judgment has started, 33
- Lament, 9
- Prayer, 16, 26
- Prayer for mercy, 78, 94
- Prophesies fulfilled, 32
- What if you are right, 91
- What if you are wrong, 91

El, 24

Elohim, Jesus as, 24

End-Times
- Deceived, 78
- Deceivers, 78

End-Times Deception
- 2 Thessalonians 1: 7-10, 28
- Trinity dogma is *the* great deception, 28

Enoch's Warning
- Enoch warns of God's punishment for changing HIS Word, 26

Equal Glory
- Trinity doctrine lie, 75

Error
- Leaders concerning God's Word, 2
- Not knowing God's power, 2
- Not knowing Scripture, 2

Eternal Life
- John 17:3, x
- Knowing God as FATHER, 9
- Knowing Jesus as Son, 9
- Knowing the God Jesus served, x

Eternals
- Trinity doctrine lie, 75

Faith and Hope
- In God HIMSELF, 35
- Through Jesus Christ, 35

Father
- Only true God, 9

FATHER is God
- Table comparing bibles, 45

Father of Lies
- John 8:44, 90

Few and Many
- Discussion, 87
- Enter by narrow gate, 91
- Matthew 7:13-14, 87

Foolish
- Hearer of God's Word, 93

Foreword, vii

Foundation
- 1 Corinthians 3:11, 106
- Jesus, Not Church, 106

Free
- To believe God's Word, 86

Freedom
- John 8:36, 86
- To discuss and challenge church doctrines suppressed, vii

Free Will
- Church doesn't respect, vii
- God respects, vii
- Revelation 22:11, vii

God
- All things are from, xi
- Comes back after Jesus, 12
- Coming to live with us, 49
- Created angel Christ, 11
- Does not have attributes that Jesus has, 18
- Doesn't change, 80
- Doesn't change like Jesus does, 18
- Do you hear HIM, vii
- Extol HIM, 8
- FATHER is only true one, 9
- Is FATHER in New Testament, 8
- Is salvation, 8
- Need to hear HIM, viii
- Not a man, 18
- Not a son of man, 18
- One God the FATHER, xi
- Rejoice before HIM, 8
- Sent Jesus, 9
- Sing praises to HIS name, 8
- Whoever hears belongs to, 90
- Whom we exist, xi
- Will he excuse Bishops, 3
- Will he excuse Cardinals, 3
- Will he excuse Pope, 3
- Will he excuse Priests, 3

God, How to know
- Psalms 45:11, 44

God, Return to HIM
- Acts 15:19, 48

God Dwells
- Isaiah 57:15, 43
- Psalms 22:3, 43

God Dwells Not
- Acts 17:24, 43

God Gives Us A Strong Mind
- 2 Timothy 1:7, 19

God Inhabits
- Psalms 22:3, 43

God Not a Man
- Numbers 23:19, 18

God Not a Son of Man
- Numbers 23:19, 18

God's Identity
- 1 Corinthians 8:6-7, 45
- 100% of bibles agree, 45
- God Is the FATHER, Table, 45

117

God's Identity (Continued)
    Jesus identifies God, xi
    Not everyone knows, 45, 47
    Paul identifies God, xi
God's Kingdom
    Location identified, 43
God's Word
    Able to save your soul, viii
    Are you listening, xi
    Doer is wise, 93
    Don't add to it, 26
    Don't alter its meaning, 26
    Don't subtract from it, 26
    First two lessons, 5
    Hearer is foolish, 93
    Is truth, 30
    Second Commandment, 39–40
    Third lesson from, 6
    Welcome it, viii
    Why isn't it important, 5
    You can understand it, viii, 103
God's Word, Hearing
    John 8:47, 34
    Not all can hear God, 34
God's Word, Receive it
    James 1:21, 102
God the FATHER
    1 Corinthians 8:6, 46
    1 Peter 1:2, 47
    1 Thessalonians 1:1, 46
    1 Timothy 1:2, 47
    2 John 1:3, 47
    2 Peter 1:17, 47
    2 Timothy 1:2, 47
    Colossians 1:12, 46
    Colossians 2:2, 46
    Ephesians 1:2, 46
    Ephesians 6:23, 46
    Galatians 1:1, 46
    Galatians 1:3, 46
    John 6:27, 46
    Jude 1:1, 47
    Philippians 2:11, 46
    Scripture search, 46–47
    Titus 1:4, 47
God the FATHER, Only
    All Orthodox churches do not know, 47
    Catholic Church does not know this fact, 47
    List of some who knew this fact, 47
    Not all know this fact, 47
God the Holy Spirit
    Idolatry, 20, 81
    Not found in Matthew 28:19, 81
God the Son
    Idolatry, 20

Gospel
    Not ashamed of it, 102

Hallelujah
    Means praise Yahweh, 8
Hear
    Peter, 35
    Thirty-three Scriptures, 34
Heart
    Surrendered, 5
Holy Father
    John 17:11, 105
    Not Peter or the Pope, 105
    Used only once in Scripture, 105
Holy Spirit
    Abides inside of us, 14
    FATHER sends in Jesus' name, 14
    Is how God dwells in us, 14
    Not Spirit of Holiness, 14
    Prayed for by Jesus, 14
    Reminds us of Jesus' teachings, 14
    Sent by FATHER only, 14
    Teaches us all things, 14
    Used by God to communicate with us, 14
    World cannot receive, 14
Holy Spirit, Poured
    Titus 3:6, 86
Home Churches
    20 Million or more now exist, 5
    Called out of Church apostasy, 5

I AM
    Context of John 8:58, 51
    Discussion - It's not Jesus, 50
Identity
    God's revealed, 8
    Jesus confirms his to Peter, 7
    Jesus says God revealed his to Peter, 7
    Where God dwells, 43
Idolatry
    Catholic Church, 3
    God the Holy Spirit, 20, 81
    God the Son, 20
    Mary Mother of God, 20
    Worship of Jesus, 2

Jesus
    Adore only Yahweh, 7
    Agree with his teachings, ix
    Angel of God, 23
    Archangel of God, 23
    As Elohim, 24
    Beginning of God's Creation, 11
    Came down to do God's will, 22
    Came from Heaven to do God's will, x
    Cannot do anything of himself, 22

Jesus (Continued)
    Can you hear him, xi
    Catholic Church concludes is God, 4
    City from my God, 10
    City of my God, 10
    Comes back before God, 12
    Coming to live with us, 49
    Confirms his true identity to Peter, 7
    Created an angel first, 11
    Created and is not eternal, 11
    Declared God's name to us, 9
    Declares doctrines are not his but God's, 22
    Declares he is a prophet, 21
    Defines the foolish person, 93
    Defines the wise person, 93
    Did nothing of his own accord, x
    Doctrine was not his, x
    Doesn't negate God's law, 50
    Don't ask of him, 24
    Don't make him a liar, 9
    Don't teach against his teachings, ix
    Do you hear him, vii, ix
    Elevated above other angels as God's Son, 11
    Eternal life was to know his God, x
    Faithful and true witness for God, 11
    First born of all creatures, 11
    First born of all creation, 11
    Fulfills the law, 50
    Fully a human man, 16
    Gives us an understanding of God, ix
    Gives us discernment, ix
    God commands us to listen to him, ix
    God dwells in him, 44
    God gave a purpose, x
    God is greater than, x
    God's Apostle, 20
    God's Prophet, 21
    Gospel he taught Paul, 48
    Had to be fully human, 16
    Had to do God's work, x
    I AM exegesis, 50
    Identifies FATHER as God, xi
    In us, 49
    I (Jesus) won't pray for you, 24
    Laid no claim to equality with God, 88
    Leads people to God, 37
    Lives by will of God, 22
    Made a man, 16
    Made better than other angels by God, 11
    Made human like all men, 16
    Made Human - Table, 89
    Made like all humans, 15
    Made like us per Hebrews 2:17, 15
    Makes us one with God, 49
    Must do God's work, 22
    Name of his God, 10
    Not Equal - Table, 89
    Not Equal - Table Notes, 90
    Not the only Son of God, 19
    One Lord Jesus Christ, xi
    Only begotten Son of God, 19
    Only did God's will, x
    Only speaks what God tells him to say, 22
    Our High Priest, 20
    Our Spiritual rock, 24
    Pray to the FATHER, 24
    Prophet who spoke for God, 30
    Rejects many Christians, 50, 92
    Salvation teaching - Jesus' last day pickup
        plan with judgment, 29
    Salvation teaching with no judgment, 29
    Saved if we know his God, ix
    Says he is Christ, Son of the living God, 7
    Says he is Son of Man, 7
    Seed of David in Flesh, 23
    Serve only Yahweh, 7
    Seven Teachings, 25
    Similar to Jeremiah, 22
    Some believe is angel Immanuel, 11
    Son of God in Spirit, 23
    Spoke God's words as any prophet would, x
    Takes vengeance on his return, 28
    Taught us to live by God's Word, 4
    Teaches against trinity, 57
    Teaches FATHER sends Holy Spirit, 14
    Teaches God's identity, 100
    Teachings are immutable, 57
    Teachings are indestructible, 57
    Temple of his God, 10
    Ten Teachings, ix
    Those who love him keep his words, 22
    Through him we believe in God, 35
    Through whom are all things, xi
    Through whom we exist, xi
    True belief turns people back to God, 37
    Used spirit words, 49
    Warning to do God's will, 58
    Warning to observe his teachings, xi
    What he taught the disciples, 100
    Who was the first of God's creation, 11
    Worship only Yahweh, 7
    You need to hear him, ix
Jesus, Agree With
    1 Timothy 6:3-4, 100
Jesus, Church Head
    1 Corinthians 12:12-27, 107
Jesus, Human
    Hebrews 2:17, 88
    Philippians 2:7, 88

Jesus (Continued)
    Jesus, Not Equal
        Philippians 2:5-12, 88
        Philippians 2:6, 88
    Jesus Angel of God
        Galatians 4:14, 23
    Jesus Archangel of God
        1 Thessalonians 4:15, 23
    Jesus' Brothers
        Matthew 12:49-50, 20
    Jesus' God
        Called YWHW, 8
        Called JEHOVAH, 8
        Called YAH, 8
        Called YAHWEH, 8
        Called YEHOVAH, 8
    Jesus' Gospel
        Acts 26:17, 48
        Converts people to God, 48
        Turns people to God, 48
    Jesus High Priest
        Hebrews 3:1-2, 20
    Jesus' Prayer
        John 17:6-8, 100
    Jesus Prophet Coming
        Deuteronomy 18:15-18, 21
    Jesus Seed of David in Flesh
        Romans 1:3, 23
    Jesus Son of God in Spirit
        Romans 1:4, 23
    Jesus Spiritual Rock
        1 Corinthians 10:1-4, 24
    Jesus' Warning
        Matthew 7:21, 58
    Judgment
        1 Peter 4:17, 33
        Begins with the Church, 33
        Bypassing God's, 56

Kingdom of God
    Inside and part of all saved people, 106
    Luke 17:20-21, 106
    Not the Catholic Church, 106
    Not in any man-made buildings, 44
King James Version
    Good reference Bible, 5
Kreeft, Peter J
    Catholic Christianity author, 79
Kyrie eleison, 94, 111

Lament
    Edward's, 9
Law Fulfillment
    Matthew 5:17-18, 50
Lessons
    First two from God's Word, 5
    Third Lesson from God's Word, 6
    Four to thirty-eight, 17
    Thirty nine to Seventy six, 27
    Seventy seven to one hundred seven, 36
    One hundred eight to one hundred sixty, 53
    Thirty three Scriptures to hear, 34
    Twenty five salvation truths, 74
    Twenty two from Roman history, 69
Lies
    From pulpit, 4
Loosed
    On earth and in Heaven, 7

Mary
    Catholic Church concludes is God's Mother, 4
    Mother of human son Jesus, 4
    Not the *only* mother of Jesus, 20
    Worshipped by Catholics, 4
Mary Mother of God
    Idolatry, 20
Mass
    Outsider's view, 43
Mind
    Brain wiring, 85
    Holy Spirit abundantly, 86
    Renew, 86
    Renewed by God's Holy Spirit, 86
    Reticular Activating System, 86
    Spiritual Rebirth, 86
Mind, Renewing
    Romans 12:2, 86
Misled
    Matthew 22:29-30, 84
Mistaken
    Leaders about God's Word, 2
    Not knowing God's Power, 2
    Not knowing Scripture, 2
Moses
    Led people to God, 37
Mothers of Jesus, Who are they
    Matthew 12:49-50, 20
Mystery of Christ
    2 Corinthians 1:13, 103
    Ephesians 3:2-4, 103
    You can understand it, viii, 103
Mythology
    Christian, 10
    Clouds God's Word, 10
    Distorts God's Word, 10

Negating God's commandments, 6
New American Bible
    Catholic Bible, 4
New King James Version
    Recommended base Bible for study, 4

New Revised Standard Version
    Generally unbiased but has nuances, 5
    Titus 2:13-14 translation error, 5
New Testament
    Doesn't negate O.T., 50
New Testament God
    Father, 8
New World Translation
    Doctrinal errors, 2
Nicene Creed, 82
Not By Faith Only
    James 2:24, 106
Notes, 108
Not Everyone Knows God's True Identity
    1 Corinthians 8:7, 47

Opinions
    Held in higher esteem than God's Word, vii
Orthodox Christianity
    Believes Jesus is God, 2
Outsider Viewpoint
    I Corinthians 14:22-23, 43
Overcome World
    Believing Jesus is Son of God, 25
    Not believing Jesus is God the Son, 25

Paraclete
    Identified as Holy Spirit, 14
    Identified as Spirit of Truth, 14
Paradise
    Enoch talks about, 56
    Is not Heaven, 56
    Luke 23:43, 56
Partiality
    Priests showed, 6
Paul
    End-Times warning, 29
    Identifies FATHER as God, xi
    Identifies one God, 13
    Identifies one Lord, 13
    Taught all things are of the FATHER, 14
    Taught all things are through Jesus Christ, 14
    Taught there is one God who is FATHER, 14
    Taught there is one Lord Jesus Christ, 14
Perish
    Did not believe God's Word, 31
    Did not believe truth, 31
    Did not love the truth, 31
Peter
    Blessed, 7
    Given keys to Heaven, 7
    Hear him, 35
Praise, Get From God
    Romans 2:28-29, 84
Praises
    God inhabits our, 43

Prayer
    Apostle Edward's, 3
    Edward's for mercy, 94
Praying
    To FATHER alone, 4
    To Mary, 4
    To saints, 4
Priest
    God makes contemptible, 6
    People seek God's law from, 6
    Should keep God's laws, 6
    Should keep knowledge, 6
    Showed partiality, 6
Progressive
    Teachers ignore teachings of Jesus, xi
Prophecy
    Mythology, 32
    Mythology and Truth prophesies fulfilled, 32
    Truth, 32
Prophecy, Mythology
    2 Timothy 4:3-4, 32
Prophecy, Truth
    2 Thessalonians 2:9-12, 32
Prophet
    False ones slain, 21
    How to recognize, 21
    Jesus declares he is a prophet, 21
    Jesus' coming prophesied, 21

Roman History
    Synopsis, 61–68
Roman Pantheon
    Roman gods, 59–60
    Summary, 61
Ruling
    Hebrews 7:1-2, 104
    King's vs. Church, 104
    Revelation 1:5-6, 104

Salvation
    Comes from God's Word, 102
    Jesus' plans for a last day pickup or free pass without judgment, 29
    None without trinity belief is a lie, 73
    Philippians 2:12, 84
    Through God's Word, 78
    Twenty five truths, 74
    Work out your own, 84
    Work out with fear and trembling, 84
Salvation Prayer, 95
Salvation Truths
    1 Corinthians 15:34, 74
    2 Timothy 3:12-15, 78
    Ezekiel 14:14, 74
    Ezekiel 18:9, 74
    Ezekiel 18:21, 74

Salvation Truths (Continue)
    Ezekiel 18:31, 74
    Joel 2:32, 74
    John 3:16, 74
    John 5:24, 74
    John 5:26, 74
    John 20:20, 74
    Luke 6:46, 74
    Matthew 5:20, 74
    Matthew 13:43, 74
    Matthew 19:17, 74
    Matthew 22:40, 74
    Psalms 3:8, 74
    Psalms 50:23, 74
    Revelation 7:10, 74
    Romans 4:8, 74
    Romans 6:22, 74
    Romans 10:10, 74
    Wisdom 5:2, 74
Scripture
    Adding a comma changes meaning, 12
    Contains everything needed to equip us, 103
    Doctrinal errors, 2
    Equips those who belong to God for good work, viii
    Errors by leaders, 2
    Few available in 325 AD, 19
    God the FATHER, 46–47
    Inspired by God, viii
    No basis for trinity doctrine, 81
    Salvation through, 78
    Study with at least three different bibles, 5
Scripture, Jewish
    Identifies God as YWHW, 17
Scripture, Misled About
    Matthew 22:29-30, 84
Seductive
    Philosophies not of Christ, xi
Set Free
    John 8:36, 86
Seven Messages
    God's End-Time Messages revealed, 3
Seven Spirits of God
    Identified in Scripture, 14
Shepherd
    Jesus, not the Pope, 107
    John 10:11, 107
    John 10:14-16, 107
    Only one, 107
Sisters of Jesus, Who Are They
    Matthew 12:49-50, 20
Social Conformity, 85
Sons of God
    Galatians 3:26, 20
    Luke 20:36, 19
    Matthew 5:9, 19
    Romans 8:14, 19
    Romans 8:19, 19
    There are many, 19
Sons of God, Who Are They
    Matthew 12:49-50, 20
Soul Stealing
    Two Church Traditions, 52
Spiritual Rebirth
    Titus 3:4-7, 86
Studying
    Avoid study bibles due to orthodox errors, 5
    Study the Word and not what men say, 5
    Use at least three bibles, 5

Teaching
    Doctrines, 7
    Man made commandments, 7
Temple of God
    1 Corinthians 3:16, 44
Tertullian
    Coins trinity word, 71
Tetragrammaton
    YWHW identifies God in Hebrew texts, 17
Textual Criticism, 13
Thomas' Exclamation
    Exegesis, 99
    John 20:27-31, 99
Those who hear God
    Belong to God, viii
Titus 2:13-14
    New Revised Standard Version error, 5
Tradition, Church
    Carved Image, 38–42
    Money Grabbing, 37–38
Traditions
    Negate God's Word, 6
Traditions, Deceiving
    Colossians 2:8, 104
Transgress
    God's command, 6
Translation
    Titus 2:13-14 Douay-Rheims' error, 12
Translation Notice, iv
Translations
    New Revised Standard Version, 5
Trinitarian Church
    Does not know God, 90
    God from God -- is a lie, 90
    Jesus was not made -- is a lie, 90
    Lies about God's Word, 90
    Serves up Satan's lies, 90
Trinity
    Created by man, 2
    Denying it threatens ingrained beliefs, 3
    No Divine revelation, 2

Trinity (Continued)
    Not in Bible, 2
Trinity Basis (Used by Church)
    1 John 4:18, 79
    Commentary, 80
    Deuteronomy 6:4, 79
    John 5:18, 79
    John 8:58, 79
    Matthew 28:19, 79
Trinity Doctrine
    1 Corinthians 8:6 refutes, 76
    Adopted in AD325, vii
    All bibles refute trinity doctrine, 76
    Athanasian Creed explains theology, 72–78
    Bible software exposes as false, 19
    Can reason with God but not the Orthodox trinity churches, 69
    Can reason with God but not the Roman Catholic Church, 69
    Catholic basis of, 79
    Catholic bibles refute teachings, 76
    Church created, 81
    Claims John 8:58 means Jesus is God, 51
    Colossians 1:15 refutes, 75
    Constantine rejects on deathbed, 70
    Contradicts Scripture, 18
    Created in context of crisis and need to unify Constantine's Roman empire, 68
    Disbelievers labeled heretics, vii
    Disbelievers persecuted, vii
    Dogma statements, 77
    Don't interpret Scripture using, 49–51
    Equal glory lie, 75
    Eternals lie, 75
    FATHER *is* greater than Jesus, 57
    Forced upon people, 69
    Hear Peter, 51
    Historical conclusion, 68
    Idiotic statements, 77
    John 6:57 refutes, 75
    John 14:28 refutes, 77
    John 20:17 refutes, 76
    Makes Jesus a liar, 9, 57
    Makes Jesus an Idiot, 57
    Mark 8:38 refutes, 75
    No basis in Scripture, 81
    No divine revelation, 66
    No salvation without trinity belief is lie, 73
    Not created in a vacuum, 68
    Pattern of deception, 77
    Philippians 3:5-6 refutes, 77
    Proverbs 8:22-31 refutes, 75
    Revelation 3:14 refutes, 75
    Teaches against what Jesus taught, 57
    They don't know God, 7
    Twenty five salvation truths refute trinity, 74
    Word smithed by lawyers and politicians, 66
Trinity Dogma
    Accepted by faith, 3
    Accepted through ignorance of Scripture, 3
    Bible software exposes, 19
    Church requires, 3
    Contradicts Scripture, 18
    Created, 2
    Created by Catholic Church, 2
    Makes Jesus a liar, 9
    Taught since 325 AD, 2
Trinity Timeline, 81
True Jew
    Romans 2:28-29, 84
Truth
    Church as pillar of, 78
    Church cannot alter God's, 30
    Church is not the basis of, 78
    Disciples abide in, 30
    Five steps to knowing, 30
    Is from God's Word, 30
    Love it or perish, 86
    They did not receive, 30
    We need to love, 30
    Will set you free, 30
Truth, Basis Of
    John 17:17, 78
    Psalms 199:160, 78
Truth, Church
    1 Timothy 3:15, 78
Truth, Knowing
    Five steps on how to, 30
    John 8:31-32, 30
Truth, Love of
    They did not receive, 31
Truth is God's Word
    John 17:17, 30
    Psalms 119:160, 30

Understanding
    Bible is written so you could understand, ix
    God's Word, ix
    Mystery of Christ, ix
    Not agreeing with Jesus source of disputes, ix
    Paul's teachings, ix
    You know nothing if you don't agree with Jesus' teachings, ix

Vain
    Worship (useless), 7
Vain Worship
    Cause of, 7
Vicar of Christ, 105

Warning
    Stay in teachings of Jesus, xi
Whoever belongs to God
    Hears HIS Word, viii
Wise
    Doer of God's Word, 93
Woe
    Edward's warning, 44
Worship
    God of the Jews, 84
    God that Jesus worshipped, 84
    How to, 84
    Idolatrous in all Orthodox churches, 3
    Idolatrous Jesus worship, 3
    In vain they, 7
    Only the FATHER, 33

Worship, FATHER
    In Spirit and truth, 33
    John 4:24, 33
Worship only God
    Matthew 4:10, 10
    Revelation 19:10, 10
    Revelation 22:8-9, 10

Yahweh
    God of Jesus, 7
    God of Jews, 7
    God of Paul, 7
    True God of Christians, 7
You can understand
    God's Word, 103
    Lord's will for you, 103
    Mystery of Christ, 103

You can understand God's Word, the Lord's will for you, and the mystery of Christ!

The Bible teaches this truth!

The Apostle Edward asks ...
Are You Ready?

When he returns for souls, will Christ find you going about God's business? Will he find your spiritual light shining? If not, why? Do you even know why Christ stated those two salvation requirements?

There is an exodus from established churches by Christians who have found out that many churches no longer teach God's truth. The trend is worldwide and was the subject of a recent newsletter I received. These Christians read the Bible and compared what their church taught. They found that the Church supported many evil things that God abhors. In the process, they have asked themselves some fundamental spiritual questions:

- Can we support abortion if God abhors the shedding of innocent blood?
- Can we support Gay rights if God says homosexuality is abominable?
- Can we support a political party that seeks to excise God from everyday life?
- Can we support world friendship when it makes us God's enemy?

Christian mythology is rampant. The *Book of Edward* discusses the above and many other important issues that the Church is now confronted with. Will you personally obey God's Word and the teachings of Jesus? If not, you are not saved. This book can reawaken your spirit and save your soul. At the very least, it will educate your heart.

I can remember the first experience in which I felt betrayed and confused by a pulpit teaching that did not line up and match what the word of God actually said. The basic choice you have, as a Christian, is whether you will adhere to God's Word or to the man made doctrines of your social group, your church, its hierarchy or its denomination.

There lies the main issue of salvation. You'll have to decide on God's Word if you want eternal life for in the end analysis you will be held accountable to HIS Word. Christians are leaving the established church and finding small fellowships or home churches as described in the New Testament. God has opened their eyes to HIS truth and if you read and study the Scriptures in this book, HE will open your eyes.

> **Jesus said: "He who rejects me, and does not receive my words, has that which judges him; the word that I have spoken will judge him in the last day." John 12:48**

If desired, you may write to me in care of Apostle Ministry, Inc. May your soul find the true salvation contained in the teachings of Jesus Christ. The Apostle Edward

Contact Apostle Edward

Apostle Edward's Contact Information

Reverend Edward G. Palmer
C/O Apostle Ministry, Inc.
18140 Zane Street NW, #410
Elk River, Minnesota 55330

Online Feedback Form

http://www.edwardtheapostle.org/feedback.html

Online Tell-A-Friend Form

http://www.edwardtheapostle.org/TAF-Form_1.html

Online Secure Donation Form

http://www.edwardtheapostle.org/donation.html

FREE NEWSLETTER

www.edwardtheapostle.org

> Do you want objective Scripture-based answers? Where Scripture itself speaks to you? Then, sign up for Apostle Edward's Free Online Newsletter. Email addresses will be validated. After you sign up, you will be asked to confirm your email.

http://www.edwardtheapostle.org/

Tell-A-Friend!

Seven End-Times Messages From God

http://www.sevenmessages.com

Trinity Dogma

http://www.trinitydogma.com

JVED PUBLISHING

www.jvedpublishing.org

Apostle Edward also wrote the —
"Book of Edward: Christian Mythology"
http://www.edwardtheapostle.org

Available Online And From All Book Stores Nationwide

You can buy the *Book of Edward* online in print form and from any bookstore including Amazon, Barnes & Noble, etc. or at http://www.edwardtheapostle.org/buythebook.html. If you buy Edward's four-volume set directly from Apostle Ministry, a free slipcase worth $59.95 will be sent to you at no charge. This slipcase is only available from Apostle Ministry, but it can be purchased if books are purchased elsewhere. You can also mail or fax your order by using the Order Form on the next page. All *Book of Edward* e-Books and e-Chapters are fully searchable PDF files and are available online at http://www.edwardtheapostle.org/esales.html. These PDF e-Book and e-Chapter files can also be ordered using the Order Form. They will be shipped to you on a CD.

Charitable Donations

Charitable donations to Apostle Ministry, Inc. are welcome and accepted. The funds received from your purchase of this book are used to support God's work. This includes buying bibles for Hindu families in India as well as supporting a ministry outreach program in India to reach unsaved souls. You can make a ministry donation online at http://www.edwardtheapostle.org/donation.html.

Book of Edward
Mail & Fax Order Form

#	Item Number	Item Description	Price	Qty	Subtotal
Printed Products					
1	ISBN 0-9798833-0-9	Book of Edward - Volume I: Matters Of The Heart	$27.95		
2	ISBN 0-9768833-1-7	Book of Edward - Volume II: God Does Not Change	$27.95		
3	ISBN 0-9768833-2-5	Book of Edward - Volume III: Itching Christian Ears	$39.95		
4	ISBN 0-9768833-3-3	Book of Edward - Volume IV: Appendixes-Reference	$27.95		
5	ISBN 0-9768833-4-1	Book of Edward - Four Volume Set (Includes Slipcase)	$123.80		
6	SLI-1	Slipcase	$59.95		
7	CGI-1	Color Graphics Set One	$19.95		
E-Book Products					
10	EBK-HC	God's Healing And Cancer - e-Book	$19.95		
11	EBK-V1	Book of Edward – Volume I - e-Book	$19.95		
12	EBK-V4	Book of Edward – Volume IV - e-Book	$14.95		
E-Chapter Products					
13	ECH-8	e-Chapter 8 – Understanding God's Word	$9.95		
14	ECH-9	e-Chapter 9 – Rationalization of Mankind	$9.95		
15	ECH-10	e-Chapter 10 – The False Trinity Doctrine	$9.95		
16	ECH-11	e-Chapter 11 – God's Eternal Character	$9.95		
17	ECH-12	e-Chapter 12 – The False Salvation Doctrine	$9.95		
18	ECH-13	e-Chapter 13 – A Light On My Path	$9.95		
19	ECH-14	e-Chapter 14 – The Gift of Jesus	$9.95		
20	ECH-15	e-Chapter 15 – Myth - God Heals Everyone	$12.95		
21	ECH-16	e-Chapter 16 – Myth - God Owns Solid Rock	$12.95		
22	ECH-17	e-Chapter 17 – Myth - Giving 10% Is A Tithe	$12.95		
23	ECH-18	e-Chapter 18 – Myth - Abortion Doesn't Matter	$12.95		
24	ECH-19	e-Chapter 19 – Myth - Sexuality Doesn't Matter	$19.95		
25	ECH-20	e-Chapter 20 – Myth - Politics Doesn't Matter	$12.95		
26	ECH-21	e-Chapter 21 – Myth - Everybody Gets To Go	$12.95		

*Include 6.875% Sales tax if state is MN. FAX ORDERS to (763) 441-7174 or Mail Orders to Apostle Ministry, Inc., 18140 Zane Street NW #410, Elk River, MN 55330. Order online at http://www.bookofedward.org. Special Bonus Offers are online only. Include all information below and provide credit card signature to authorize charge.

Sales Tax*	
Shipping	$15.00
Total	

Returns: **30-Day Money Back Guarantee on printed products.** *All E-Book and E-Chapter sales are final.*

Credit Card: Discover____ Visa____ MasterCard____ American Express____ My Check Is Enclosed____

Card Name: _____ Card No: _____

Card Expires: _____ Card Security Code: _____ Email: _____

Ship Name: _____ Address: _____

City: _____ State: _____ Zip: _____ Phone: _____

Date: _____ Signature: _____

Copyright Notice

Thank you for purchasing "Trinity Dogma - The Book." Copyright laws protect this written work of Reverend Edward G. Palmer. Distribution to others in any form is a violation of copyright laws. Volume discounts are available. Contact the author for further details. Thank you for respecting copyright laws. God will bless your honesty. This work is a ministry to Christians with God's message that they need to love HIS Word more than they love the doctrines of their Church. Your support will help save souls, especially Christian souls that are now lost to Church dogma and who no longer are in love with God's Word. This is God's book and is being used by HIM to get a critical message out to Christ's Bride, the Church!

Copyright 2009
Rev. Edward G. Palmer
All Rights Reserved

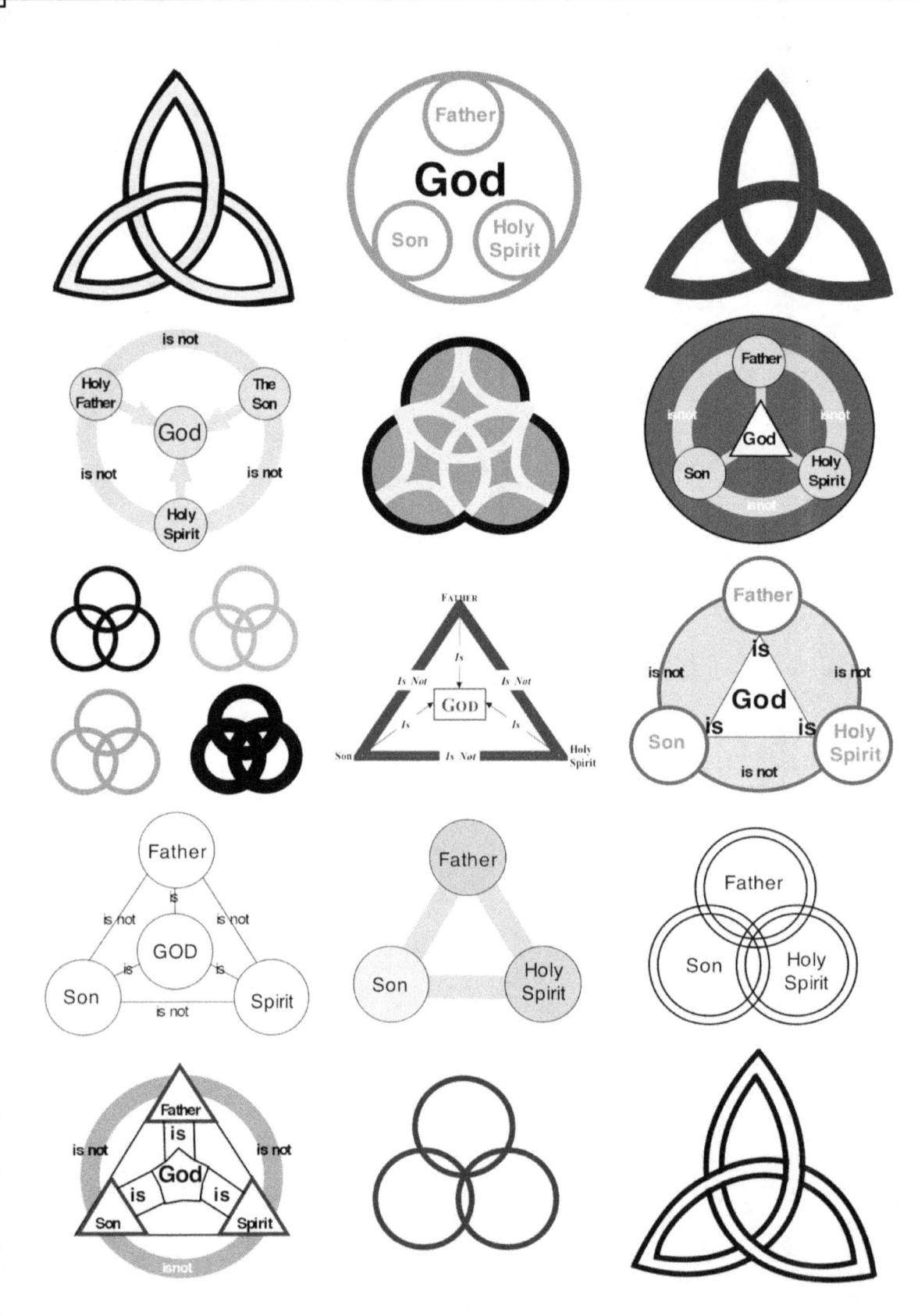

www.ingramcontent.com/pod-product-compliance
Lightning Source LLC
Chambersburg PA
CBHW082125230426
43671CB00015B/2805